RECENT HISTORY ATLAS

Also by Martin Gilbert

Jewish History Atlas
British History Atlas
American History Atlas
The Roots of Appeasement
The European Powers
The Appeasers (*with Richard Gott*)
Winston Churchill (Clarendon Biographies)

Editions of documents

Britain and Germany Between the Wars
Plough My Own Furrow: the Life of Lord Allen of Huntwood
Servant of India: Diaries of the Viceroy's Private Secretary 1905–1910
Churchill (*Spectrum Books*)
Lloyd George (*Spectrum Books*)

Recent History Atlas 1860 to 1960

Martin Gilbert
Fellow of Merton College, Oxford

Cartography by JOHN R. FLOWER

Weidenfeld and Nicolson
5 Winsley Street, London, W1

Printed Offset Litho in Great Britain by
Cox & Wyman Ltd., London, Fakenham and Reading

Preface

The maps in this atlas aim to present the main historical
developments from 1860 to 1960. Each map has been
specially designed to help explain some important episode in recent
history. Each continent is given as much importance as the events
determine; not only wars and battles, but also treaties, alliances,
population problems and political confrontations are the subject of
these maps. I have consulted a wide range of existing atlases,
reference books, newspaper files, and specialized historical works.
These sources have provided the statistical and factual information
which can be usefully brought together on a map. My aim has been
to help the reader grasp at once a wide range of relevant historical
points, as clearly and accurately as possible.
My thanks go to all those who have helped improve the maps by
their suggestions; in particular to Mr. John Emerson, Miss Joanna
Kaye, Mr. Michael Perman, Dr. John Roberts, and Miss Maureen
Turnbull.
I should also like to thank those who have sent me corrections
since the first English edition was published in August 1966, and
have thereby greatly improved the accuracy of the Atlas:
Mr. John M. Austen, Mr. T. F. R. G. Braun, Mr. Lance Brown,
Mr. Frank Gannon, Mr. I. M. Gillies, Mr. Tosco Fyvel, Professor
Michael Roberts, Lieutenant-Commander A. G. Thomas, R.N.,
Mr. Alexander Werth, Sir John Wheeler-Bennett and
Mr. Michael St. J. Wright.
I should welcome any further corrections for future editions.

MARTIN GILBERT
Merton College, Oxford

1967

List of Maps

	GREAT BRITAIN	GERMANY	FRANCE	ITALY	U.S.A.	RUSSIA	OTHER NATIONS
1860	1867 Occupies Bahrein MAP 12 1869 Occupies Nicobar Islands MAP 19	1866 Defeats Austria MAP 4	1860 Gains Nice and Savoy MAP 3 1863 Gains Cambodia MAP 17 & 119	1860 Garibaldi enters Palermo MAP 3 1866 Fleet destroyed by Austria MAP 3 1866 Gains Venice MAP 5 & 3	1861 Civil War begins MAP 11 1865 Confederates surrender; Lincoln assassinated MAP 11	1860 Annexes Vladivostok MAP 17 1868 Occupies Samarkand MAP 12	1863 Greeks gain Corfu MAP 13 1866 Austria loses Venice MAP 5
1870	1874 Protectorate over Malaya MAP 17 1878 Occupies Cyprus MAP 7	1870 Besieges Paris MAP 2 1871 Annexes Alsace-Lorraine MAP 4	1870 Attacks Germany MAP 2 1871 Defeated by Germany MAP 2	1870 Final unification MAP 3 1871 Rome made capital MAP 3		1873 Occupies Khiva and Bukhara MAP 12 1877 Declares war on Turkey MAP 8 1878 Occupies Kars MAP 7 1878 Defeats Turks MAP 8	1876 Turks massacre Bulgarians MAP 8 1878 Austria occupies Bosnia MAP 5
1880	1882 Occupies Egypt MAP 7 1886 Occupies Upper Burma MAP 17	1884 Colony in South West Africa MAP 16	1881 Occupies Tunisia MAP 7 1884 Gains Annam MAP 17	1889 Colony in East Africa MAP 16		1887 Occupies Penjdeh MAP 12	
1890	1890 Occupies Quetta MAP 12 1898 Dervishes defeated at Omdurman MAP 20 1899 Protects Kuwait MAP 12 1899 Attacked by Boers MAP 15	1890 Colony in East Africa MAP 16	1893 Gains Laos MAP 17 & 119 1898 Sphere of influence in Siam MAP 17 & 119		1898 Gains Philippines from Spain MAP 17 1898 Occupies Cuba MAP 104		1895 Japan annexes Formosa MAP 17
1900	1902 Boers surrender MAP 15 1904 Defeats Tibetans MAP 12 1907 Extends influence over Persia MAP 12	1909 Plan to invade France through neutral Belgium MAP 26			1900 Decade of most intense immigration begins MAP 10 1909 Occupies Nicaragua MAP 104	1905 Defeated by Japan MAP 18 1907 Extends influence over Persia MAP 12	1905 Japan defeats Russia MAP 18
1910 / **1920**	1910 Churchill at German Army manoeuvres MAP 20 1914 Army helps France to resist German attack MAP 25 1915 Attempts to defeat Turkey at Dardanelles MAP 33 1916 Vast losses for tiny gains at Battle of the Somme MAP 38 1918 Defeats Germany MAP 30 1918 Intervenes in Russian Civil War MAP 39	1914 Vast expenditure on military preparation MAP 22 1914 Attacks Belgium and France MAP 25 1914 Defeats Russians at Tannenberg MAP 31 1916 Fleet checked at Jutland MAP 38 1918 Defeated MAP 30 1918 War Deaths MAP 38	1915 Trench warfare across Eastern France MAP 27 1917 Relief force sent to help Italy MAP 29 1918 Regains Alsace-Lorraine MAP 30	1912 Conquers Libya MAP 7 1914 Neutral on outbreak of War MAP 24 1917 Defeated by Austria at Caporetto MAP 29 1919 Gains Istria and Tyrol MAP 3	1916 Occupies Dominican Republic MAP 104 1917 Enters World War MAP 23 1918 Troops active against Germany MAP 30 1918 Intervenes in Russian Civil War MAP 39	1914 Initial victory against Germany MAP 31 1915 Driven back by Germany MAP 32 1917 Cedes territory to Germany MAP 37 1917 High number of War deaths MAP 38 1918 Civil War MAP 39	1913 Turks driven from Balkans MAP 13 1914 Liberia and Abyssinia only two independent African States MAP 14 1914 Austrians driven back by Russians MAP 31 1915 Serbia defeated MAP 32 1917 China and Brazil join World War MAP 23 1917 Austria advances towards Venice MAP 29 1918 Turkey defeated MAP 35 1918 Bulgaria defeated MAP 36

	GREAT BRITAIN	GERMANY	FRANCE	ITALY	U.S.A.	RUSSIA	OTHER NATIONS
1920		1920 Loses large part of Silesia MAP 44 1922 Retains East Prussia MAP 62 1923 Hitler fails to seize power in Munich MAP 49		1921 Becomes dictatorship MAP 48	1926 Occupies Nicaragua MAP 104	1920 Fails to conquer Poland MAP 40	1920 Poles drive Russians back from Warsaw MAP 40 1920 Poland a State with many minorities MAP 61 1922 Turks defeat Greeks MAP 42 1926 Poland becomes dictatorship MAP 48
1930	1935 Plan to partition Abyssinia MAP 51 1939 Guarantees Poland, Greece, Rumania & Turkey MAP 65	1930 First Nazi election successes MAP 49 1935 Gains Saar by Plebiscite MAP 50 1938 Annexes Austria MAP 50 1938 Gains territory from Czechoslovakia MAP 53 1939 Air Force largest in the World MAP 63 1939 Invades Poland MAP 64		1935 Invades Abyssinia MAP 51 1936 Pact of Steel with Germany MAP 65 1939 Occupies Albania MAP 56		1939 Non-aggression pact with Germany MAP 65 1939 Occupies Eastern Poland MAP 64 1939 Expelled from League of Nations MAP 47	1931 Japan invades Manchuria MAP 52 1936 Spanish Civil War begins MAP 55 1937 Japan occupies Peking MAP 52 1938 Hungary gains Czechoslovak territory MAP 46 1938 Czechoslovakia loses vital industry & defences MAP 54 1939 Poland partitioned MAP 59 1939 Russia invades Finland MAP 66
1940	1940 Driven from Norway by Germans MAP 67 1940 Bombed by Germans MAP 69 1941 Attempts to resist Germans in Greece MAP 70 1943 Invades Italy MAP 79 1944 Plans invasion of Hitlers Europe MAP 82 1944 Normandy Landings MAP 83 1945 Churchill crosses the Rhine MAP 92 1947 Leaves India MAP 100 1948 Leaves Palestine MAP 102	1940 Occupies Paris MAP 68 1941 Occupies parts of Slovenia & Serbia MAP 56 1941 Invades Greece MAP 70 1941-1945 Murders Jews MAP 86 1942 Reaches Stalingrad MAP 72 1943-1945 Cities bombed MAP 84 1945 Dresden destroyed MAP 85 1945 Surrenders MAP 87 1945 Germans expelled from Central Europe MAP 89 1945 Occupied by victors MAP 94 1945 Berlin partitioned MAP 117 & 118	1940 Defeated by Germany MAP 68 1943 Resistance Movement in Corsica MAP 79 1945 Paris liberated MAP 87 1949 A member of NATO MAP 116	1941 Invades Greece MAP 56 1943 Surrenders to allied nations MAP 79	1940 Leases British bases in return for bombers MAP 73 1941 Sends Lend-lease to allied nations MAP 75 1941 Attacked by Japan MAP 52 1942 Naval victories against Japan MAP 90 1943 Invades Italy MAP 79 1944 Normandy Landings MAP 83 1945 Defeats Japan MAP 91 1945 Occupies Japan MAP 101	1941 Invaded by Germany MAP 71 1941 Leningrad besieged MAP 80 1942 Drives out Germans MAP 81 1945 Immense toll of war MAP 93 1945 Gains Bessarabia MAP 58 1945 Annexes Eastern Poland MAP 60 1946 Establishes economic block in Eastern Europe MAP 111	1940 Germany invades Holland, Belgium and France MAP 71 1941 Germany invades Yugoslavia and Greece MAP 70 1941 Hungary gains Rumanian territory MAP 46 1941 Japan attacks British, French & U.S. territory in the Pacific MAP 52 1941 Britain liberates Abyssinia MAP 77 1942 Japan occupies Singapore MAP 90 1945 The immense toll of the war MAP 93 1945-1948 Advance of communism in Eastern Europe MAP 94 1947 Civil war between India and Pakistan MAP 100 1948 Arab-Jewish War MAP 102
1950	1956 Attacks Suez Canal MAP 103		1954 Defeated in Indo-China MAP 119	1954 Retains Trieste but not Istria MAP 99	1950 Main United Nations participant in Korean War MAP 106 & 107	1955 Establishes defensive Warsaw Pact MAP 116	1950 Communist Revolution in China MAP 101 1950 Korean War MAP 106 & 107 1956 United Nations intervenes after Suez War MAP 103 1957 European Common Market established MAP 111
1960	1961 Oil interests in Middle East MAP 112	1960 Divided Germany an area of east-west conflict MAP 116			1960 Negroes MAP 109 1962 Blockades Cuba MAP 105 1963 Signs Test Ban Treaty MAP 110 1964 New York's population MAP 114 1965 Active in Vietnam War MAP 120	1960 Shoots down U.S. spy plane over central Russia MAP 121 1962 Establishes missile bases in Cuba MAP 105 1964 Chinese claim territory from MAP 108	1960 The rapid spread of African independence MAP 98 1960 United Nations active in the Congo MAP 97 1963 Nuclear Test Ban Treaty signed in Moscow MAP 110 1964 China explodes her first atomic device MAP 108 1965 War between India and Pakistan MAP 116
1970							

NORWAY
AND
SWEDEN

FINLAND

○ St. Petersburg

North Sea

Baltic Sea

○ Riga

Moscow ○

DENMARK

Heligoland (British) •

RUSSIAN
EMPIRE

○ Königsberg

EAST PRUSSIA

NETHERLANDS

Berlin ○

GERMANY
Empire proclaimed in January 1871

SILESIA

○ Warsaw

POLAND

○ Kiev

BELGIUM

○ Paris

LUXEMBURG

FRENCH
EMPIRE

○ Prague

BAVARIA

Munich ○

GALICIA

○ Cracow

HABSBURG

UKRAINE

BESSARABIA

Odessa ○

SWITZERLAND

Vienna ○

Budapest ○

EMPIRE

ITALY

Trieste ○

Adriatic Sea

RUMANIA
Autonomous

○ Bucharest

○ Belgrade

SERBIA
Autonomous

BULGARIA
Autonomous

Black Sea

BOSNIA

CORSICA
(French)

Rome ○

SARDINIA
(Italian)

MONTE-
NEGRO

Sofia ○

Constantinople ○

OTTOMAN

EMPIRE

Corfu
(Greek)

GREECE

The EUROPEAN
EMPIRES in 1870
Before the Franco Prussian war

Miles

0 — 100 — 200 — 300

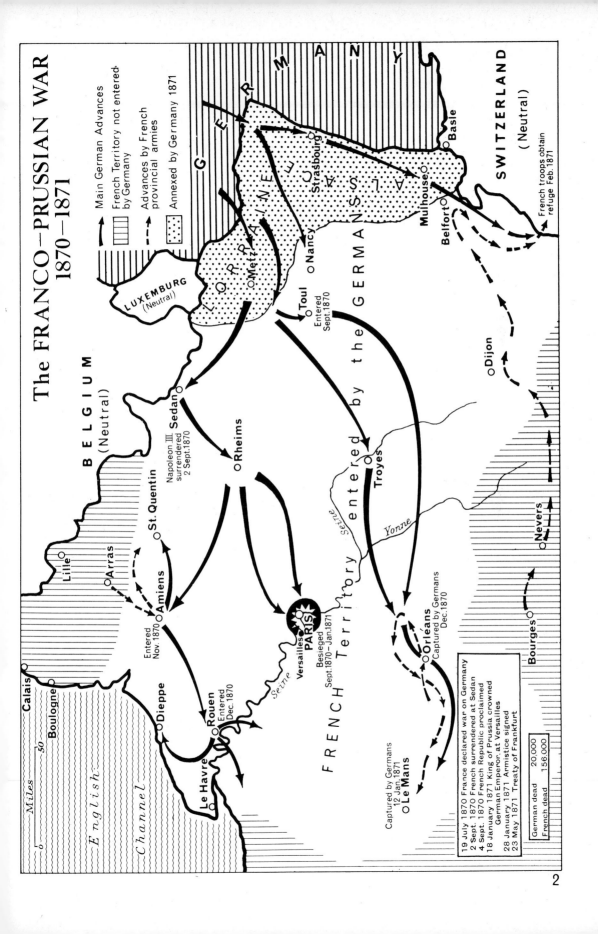

The FRANCO–PRUSSIAN WAR 1870–1871

Main German Advances
French Territory not entered by Germany
Advances by French provincial armies
Annexed by Germany 1871

GERMANY

SWITZERLAND (Neutral)

French troops obtain refuge Feb. 1871

Basle

Strasbourg
Mulhouse

A L S A C E

Belfort

L O R R A I N E

Nancy

Metz

LUXEMBURG (Neutral)

Toul
Entered Sept.1870

Dijon

BELGIUM (Neutral)

Sedan
Napoleon III surrendered 2 Sept.1870

Rheims

entered by the GERMANS

Troyes

Yonne

St. Quentin

Lille

Arras

Amiens
Entered Nov. 1870

PARIS
Versailles
Besieged Sept.1870–Jan.1871

Seine

F R E N C H   T e r r i t o r y

Orleans
Captured by Germans Dec.1870

Nevers

Calais

Boulogne

Dieppe

Rouen
Entered Dec. 1870

Le Havre

Seine

English Channel

Miles
0   50

Captured by Germans 12 Jan. 1871

Le Mans

Bourges

19 July 1870 France declared war on Germany
2 Sept. 1870 French surrendered at Sedan
4 Sept. 1870 French Republic proclaimed
18 January 1871 King of Prussia crowned German Emperor at Versailles
28 January 1871 Armistice signed
23 May 1871 Treaty of Frankfurt

German dead   20,000
French dead   156,000

2

Germany

Austria - Hungary

Switzerland

France

TYROL

SAVOY
(to France)
1860

K
I
N
G

LOMBARDY
1859

Magenta ⊗
1859
○ Milan
Solferino ⊗
1859

VENETIA
1866

⊗ Verona
Custozza ⊗
1866

Trieste ○

○ Verona

Venice ○

ISTRIA

Fiume ○

○ Turin

PIEDMONT

PARMA
1860

R. Po

Dalmatia

Ottoman
Empire

D
O
M

NICE
(to France)
1860

○ Genoa

MONACO Independent.
Sardinian Protection
1815-1860.
French Protection since
1861.

MODENA
1860

ROMAGNA
1860

SAN MARINO
(Ind. Rep.)

MARCHES
1860

Castelfidardo ⊗
1860

Adriatic

Lissa
1866 ⤬
Austrians destroy
Italian fleet

O
F

○ Florence
Capital of Italy
1864-1871

TUSCANY
1860

PAPAL
STATES

UMBRIA
1860

Sea

Lagosta
(Italian until
1919)

(PIEDMONT)

Corsica
(French)

● Elba

THE
PATRIMONY
1870

Mentana
⊗ Garibaldi defeated
by the French
3 November
1867

N

BENEVENTO
(Papal
to 1860)

A

Tyrrhenian

ROME
Entered by
Italians 1870.
Made Italian Capital
1871.

Gaeta ⊗
1861

Entered by Garibaldi
7 September 1860

○ Naples

P

SARDINIA

Sea

KINGDOM

OF THE

TWO SICILIES
1860

L

1852 Cavour, Premier
of Piedmont.
1861 Victor Emmanuel
King of Italy.

Entered by Garibaldi
6 June 1860

E

S

Mediterranean

Aspromonte
⊗ Garibaldi captured
29 August 1862

○ Palermo

S I C I L Y

T U N I S I A

(Part of OTTOMAN
EMPIRE)

Sea

Dates refer to
Union with Piedmont

▥ Italian gains in 1919

The
UNIFICATION of ITALY
1859 – 1870
with gains of 1919

Miles
0   50   100

3

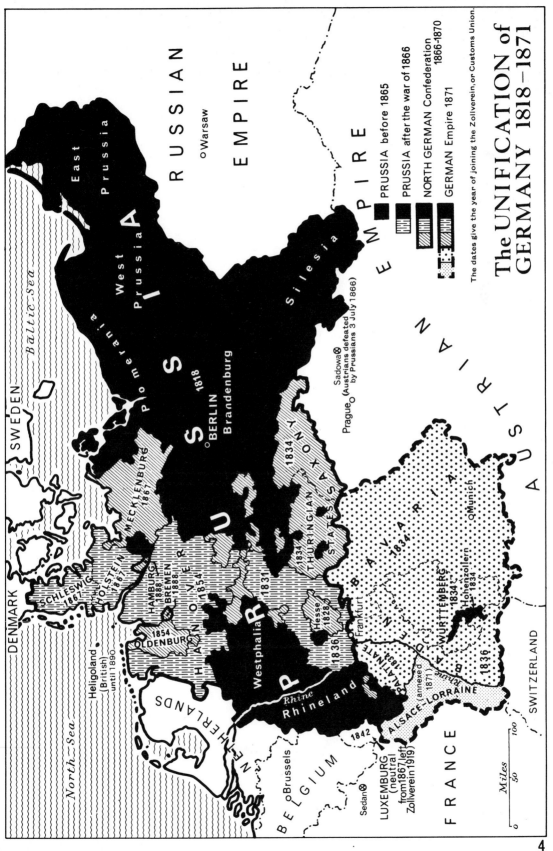

The UNIFICATION of GERMANY 1818–1871

The dates give the year of joining the Zollverein, or Customs Union.

- ■ PRUSSIA before 1865
- ▨ PRUSSIA after the war of 1866
- ▤ NORTH GERMAN Confederation 1866-1870
- ▨ GERMAN Empire 1871

RUSSIAN EMPIRE

AUSTRIAN EMPIRE

SWEDEN

DENMARK

Baltic Sea

North Sea

Heligoland (British) until 1890

SCHLESWIG 1867

HOLSTEIN 1867

MECKLENBURG 1867

East Prussia

West Prussia

Pomerania

Silesia

o Warsaw

BERLIN 1818

Brandenburg

Prague o

Sadowa ⊗ (Austrians defeated by Prussians 3 July 1866)

HAMBURG 1888

BREMEN 1888

HANOVER 1854

OLDENBURG 1854

Hesse 1828

THURINGIAN STATES 1834

SAXONY 1834

Frankfurt

PRUSSIA

Westphalia

Rhineland

Rhine

NETHERLANDS

BELGIUM

Brussels o

Sedan ⊗

LUXEMBURG (neutral from 1867, left Zollverein 1919)

1842

BAVARIA 1834

WÜRTTEMBERG 1834

Hohenzollern 1834

BADEN 1836

1834

o Munich

PALATINATE 1834

ALSACE-LORRAINE (annexed 1871)

FRANCE

SWITZERLAND

Miles
0   50   100

4

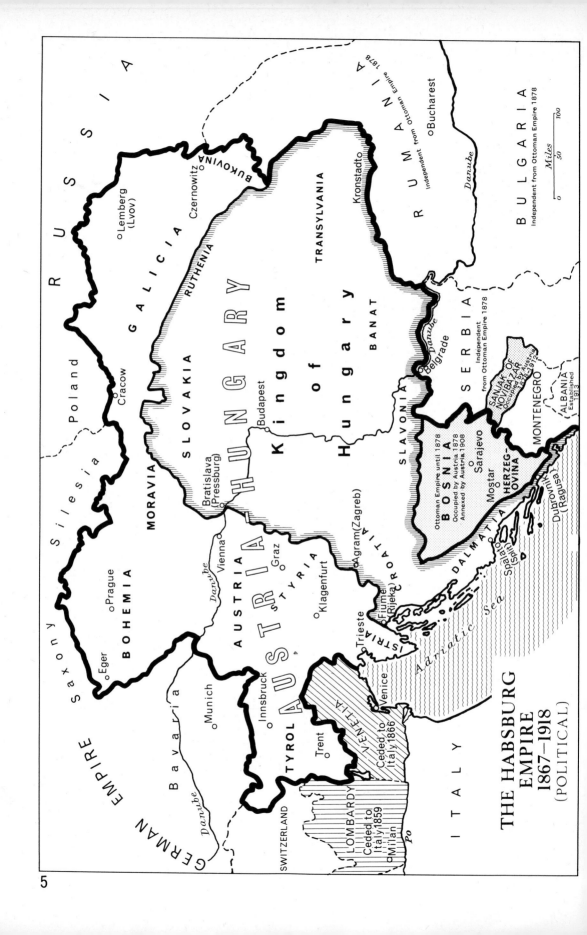

THE HABSBURG EMPIRE 1867–1918 (POLITICAL)

GERMAN EMPIRE

RUSSIA

Poland

Silesia

Saxony

Bavaria

SWITZERLAND

ITALY

BOHEMIA
Eger o
Prague o

MORAVIA

GALICIA
Cracow o
Lemberg (Lvov) o

RUTHENIA
Czernowitz o

BUKOVINA

SLOVAKIA

Bratislava (Pressburg) o

Budapest o

Kingdom of Hungary

TRANSYLVANIA
Kronstadt o

BANAT

RUMANIA
Independent from Ottoman Empire 1878
Bucharest o
Danube

BULGARIA
Independent from Ottoman Empire 1878

Miles
0   50   100

AUSTRIA
Vienna o
Danube
STYRIA
Graz o
Klagenfurt o

Innsbruck o
TYROL
Trent o

VENETIA
Ceded to Italy 1866
Venice o
Trieste o
ISTRIA

LOMBARDY
Ceded to Italy 1859
Milan o
Po

Danube

Agram (Zagreb) o
CROATIA
SLAVONIA

Fiume (Rijeka) o

Belgrade o
Danube

SERBIA
Independent from Ottoman Empire 1878

BOSNIA
Ottoman Empire until 1878
Occupied by Austria 1878
Annexed by Austria 1908
Sarajevo o

HERZEG-OVINA
Mostar o

DALMATIA
Spalato (Split) o
Dubrovnik (Ragusa) o

Adriatic Sea

SANJAK OF NOVIBAZAR
Occupied by Austria 1872–1913

MONTENEGRO

ALBANIA
Established 1913

5

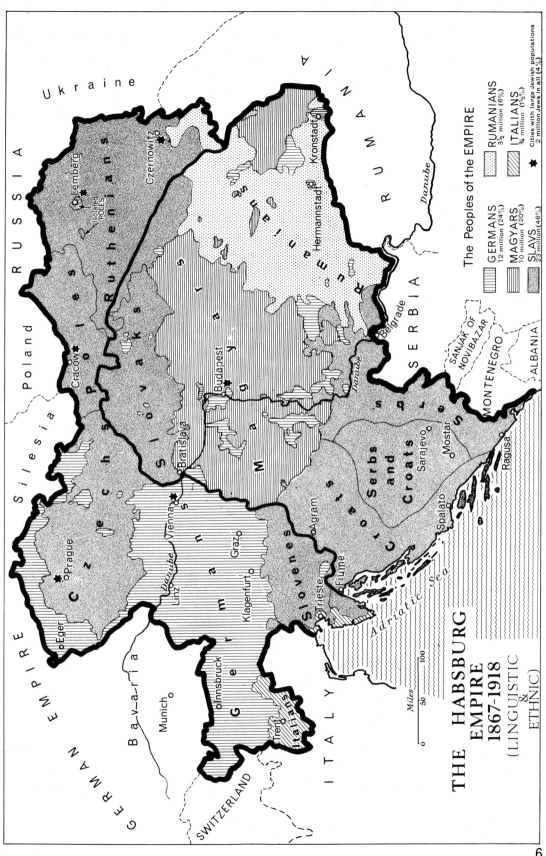

THE HABSBURG
EMPIRE
1867-1918
(LINGUISTIC
&
ETHNIC)

The Peoples of the EMPIRE

GERMANS 12 million (24%)	RUMANIANS 3½ million (6%)
MAGYARS 10 million (20%)	ITALIANS ¾ million (1½%)
SLAVS 23 million (46%)	★ Cities with large Jewish populations 2 million Jews in all (4%)

Miles
0   50   100

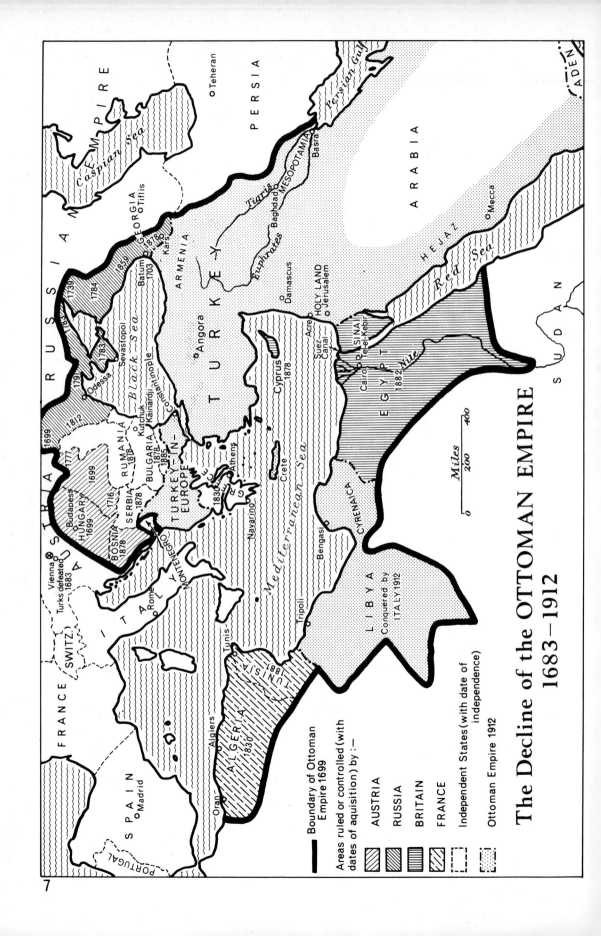

The Decline of the OTTOMAN EMPIRE
1683–1912

Boundary of Ottoman Empire 1699

Areas ruled or controlled (with dates of aquisition) by :—

AUSTRIA

RUSSIA

BRITAIN

FRANCE

Independent States (with date of independence)

Ottoman Empire 1912

Miles
0   200   400

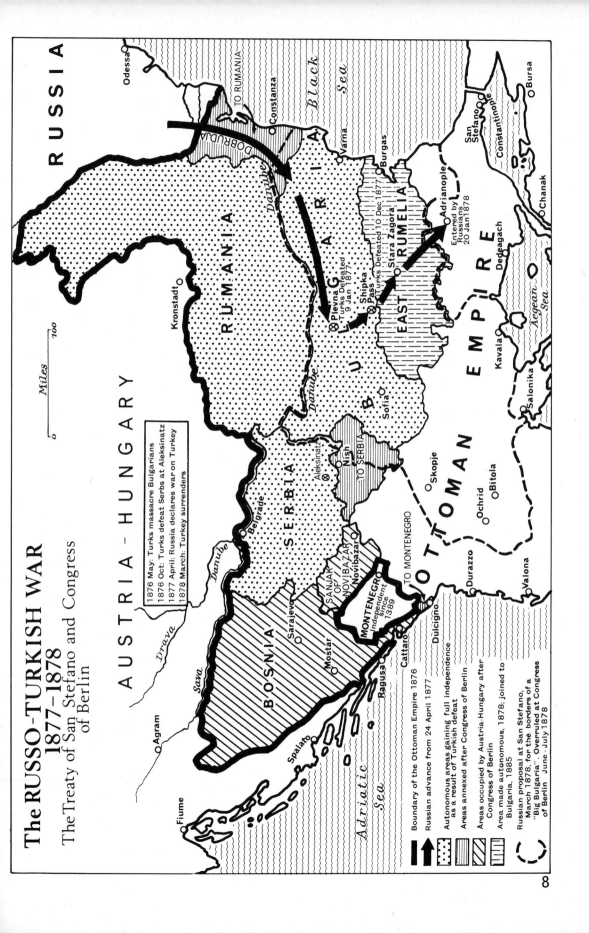

The RUSSO-TURKISH WAR
1877–1878
The Treaty of San Stefano and Congress of Berlin

1876 May: Turks massacre Bulgarians
1876 Oct: Turks defeat Serbs at Aleksinatz
1877 April: Russia declares war on Turkey
1878 March: Turkey surrenders

Boundary of the Ottoman Empire 1876

Russian advance from 24 April 1877

Autonomous areas gaining full independence
as a result of Turkish defeat

Areas annexed after Congress of Berlin

Areas occupied by Austria-Hungary after
Congress of Berlin

Area made autonomous, 1878; joined to
Bulgaria, 1885

Russian proposal at San Stefano,
March 1878, for the borders of a
"Big Bulgaria". Overruled at Congress
of Berlin June-July 1878

RUSSIA

Odessa

Black Sea

TO RUMANIA

Constanza

DOBRUDJA

Danube

Varna

Burgas

B U L G A R I A

Plevna
Turks Defeated
9 Jan 1877

Shipka
Pass

Turks Defeated 10 Dec 1877

Stara Zagora

EAST RUMELIA

San Stefano

Constantinople

Adrianople
Entered by
Russians
20 Jan 1878

Bursa

Chanak

Dedeagach

Aegean Sea

Kavala

Salonika

OTTOMAN EMPIRE

Sofia

Nish

TO SERBIA

Skopje

Ochrid

Bitola

Durazzo

Valona

Aleksinatz

SERBIA

Belgrade

Kronstadt

RUMANIA

Danube

AUSTRIA-HUNGARY

Agram

Fiume

Drava

Sava

Danube

Spalato

BOSNIA

Sarajevo

Mostar

Ragusa

SANJAK
OF
NOVIBAZAR
Novibazar

MONTENEGRO
Independent
since
1389

TO MONTENEGRO

Cattaro

Dulcigno

Adriatic Sea

Miles
0   100

8

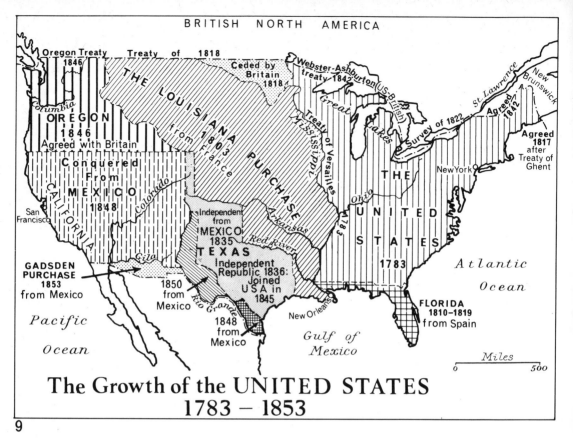

BRITISH NORTH AMERICA

Oregon Treaty 1846
Treaty of 1818
Ceded by Britain 1818
Webster-Ashburton treaty 1842 (US-British)
St. Lawrence
New Brunswick
Columbia
OREGON 1846
Agreed with Britain
THE LOUISIANA PURCHASE from France 1803
Treaty of Versailles
Great Lakes
Survey of 1822
Agreed 1842
Agreed 1817 after Treaty of Ghent
Conquered From MEXICO 1848
Colorado
Mississippi
THE UNITED STATES 1783
New York
San Francisco
CALIFORNIA
Arkansas
Ohio
Atlantic Ocean
GADSDEN PURCHASE 1853 from Mexico
Gila
Independent from MEXICO 1835
TEXAS Independent Republic 1836: Joined USA in 1845
Red River
1783
1850 from Mexico
Rio Grande
1848 from Mexico
New Orleans
FLORIDA 1810-1819 from Spain
Pacific Ocean
Gulf of Mexico
Miles 0 500

The Growth of the UNITED STATES
1783 – 1853

9

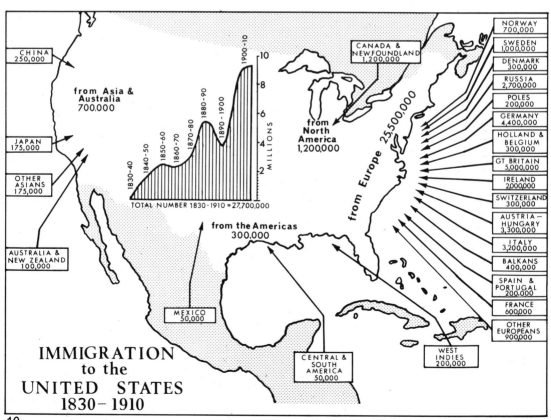

CHINA 250,000

from Asia & Australia 700.000

CANADA & NEWFOUNDLAND 1,200,000

JAPAN 175,000

from North America 1,200,000

OTHER ASIANS 175,000

from Europe 25,500,000

1900-10
1890-1900
1880-90
1870-80
1860-70
1850-60
1840-50
1830-40

10
8
6
4
2
MILLIONS

TOTAL NUMBER 1830-1910 = 27,700,000

from the Americas 300,000

AUSTRALIA & NEW ZEALAND 100,000

MEXICO 50,000

CENTRAL & SOUTH AMERICA 50,000

WEST INDIES 200,000

NORWAY 700,000
SWEDEN 1,000,000
DENMARK 300,000
RUSSIA 2,700,000
POLES 200,000
GERMANY 4,400,000
HOLLAND & BELGIUM 300,000
GT BRITAIN 5,000,000
IRELAND 2,000,000
SWITZERLAND 300,000
AUSTRIA – HUNGARY 3,300,000
ITALY 3,200,000
BALKANS 400,000
SPAIN & PORTUGAL 200,000
FRANCE 600,000
OTHER EUROPEANS 900,000

IMMIGRATION to the UNITED STATES
1830 – 1910

10

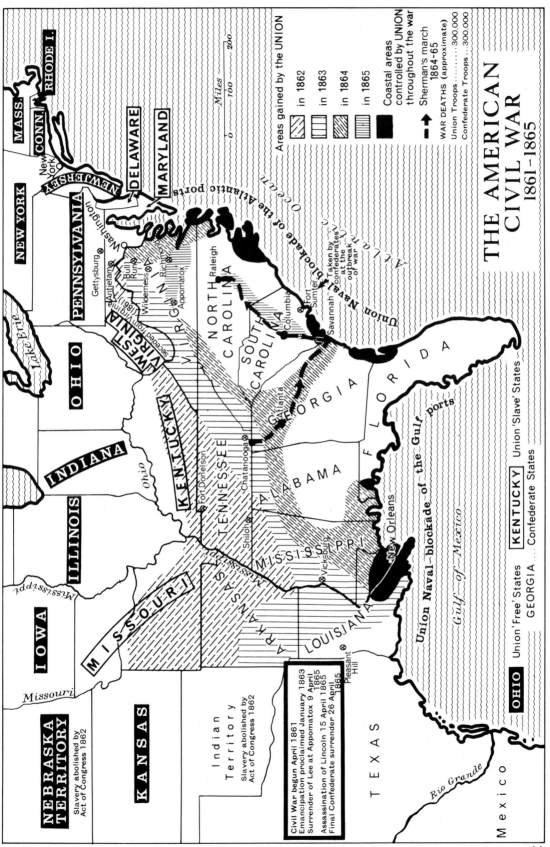

THE AMERICAN CIVIL WAR
1861–1865

Areas gained by the UNION

in 1862

in 1863

in 1864

in 1865

Coastal areas controlled by UNION throughout the war

Sherman's march 1864–65

WAR DEATHS (approximate)
Union Troops..........300,000
Confederate Troops...300,000

OHIO Union 'Free' States

KENTUCKY Union 'Slave' States

GEORGIA Confederate States

Civil War begun April 1861
Emancipation proclaimed January 1863
Surrender of Lee at Appomatox 9 April 1865
Assassination of Lincoln 15 April 1865
Final Confederate surrender 26 April 1865

NEBRASKA TERRITORY
Slavery abolished by Act of Congress 1862

KANSAS

Indian Territory
Slavery abolished by Act of Congress 1862

IOWA

MISSOURI

ILLINOIS

INDIANA

OHIO

NEW YORK

PENNSYLVANIA

WEST VIRGINIA seceded from Virginia 1861

VIRGINIA

KENTUCKY

TENNESSEE

ARKANSAS

MISSISSIPPI

ALABAMA

GEORGIA

NORTH CAROLINA

SOUTH CAROLINA

FLORIDA

LOUISIANA

TEXAS

Mexico

MASS.
CONN.
RHODE I.
NEW JERSEY
DELAWARE
MARYLAND

New York
Washington
Gettysburg
Antietam
Bull Run
Wilderness
Richmond
Appomatox
Raleigh
Columbia
Fort Sumter
Taken by Confederates at the outbreak of war
Savannah
Atlanta
Chattanooga
Fort Donelson
Shiloh
Vicksburg
New Orleans
Pleasant Hill

Union Naval blockade of the Atlantic ports

Union Naval blockade of the Gulf ports

Atlantic Ocean

Gulf of Mexico

Lake Erie

Ohio

Mississippi

Missouri

Rio Grande

Miles
0 100 200

11

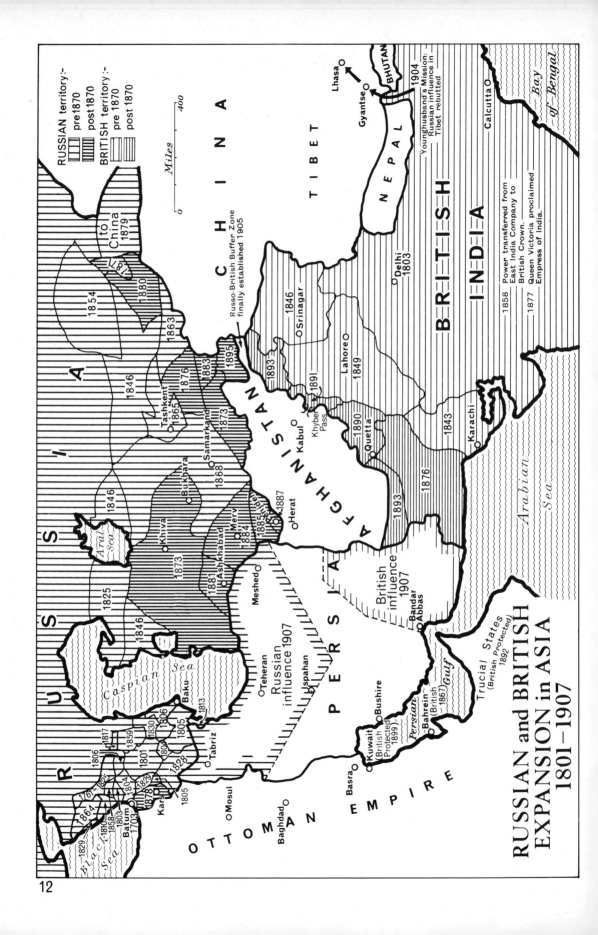

RUSSIAN and BRITISH
EXPANSION in ASIA
1801–1907

RUSSIAN territory:-
pre1870
post 1870
BRITISH territory:-
pre 1870
post 1870

Miles
0   400

R U S S I A

C H I N A

to
China
1879

1854

1880

1863

1846

1846

1846

1846

1846

1825

Aral
Sea

Tashkent
1865

Samarkand
1868

Bukhara

Khiva
1873

Merv
1884

Ashkhabad
1881

1876

1883

1895

1873

1885

1884

1885

Herat
1887

Russo-British Buffer Zone
finally established 1905

T I B E T

Lhasa

Gyantse

NEPAL

1904   Younghusband's Mission:
Russian influence in
Tibet rebutted

BHUTAN

Bay
of Bengal

Calcutta

B R I T I S H

I N D I A

1858   Power transferred from
East India Company to
British Crown.
1877   Queen Victoria proclaimed
Empress of India.

Srinagar
1846

Delhi
1803

Lahore
1849

1893

1891

Khyber
Pass

Kabul

A F G H A N I S T A N

1890

Quetta

1876

1893

1876

1843

Karachi

Arabian
Sea

Meshed

Russian
influence 1907

British
influence
1907

Bandar
Abbas

Trucial States
(British Protected)
1892

P E R S I A

Teheran

Ispahan

Caspian   Sea

Baku
1813

1830

1806

1805

1859

1805

1801

1804

1828

1806

1817

1829

1805

Tabriz

Kars
1878

Batum
1878

Black   Sea

1703

1761

1810

1805

1858

1803

1829

1864

Mosul

Baghdad

Basra

Kuwait
British
Protected
1899

Bushire

Bahrein
(British)
1867

Persian   Gulf

O T T O M A N   E M P I R E

12

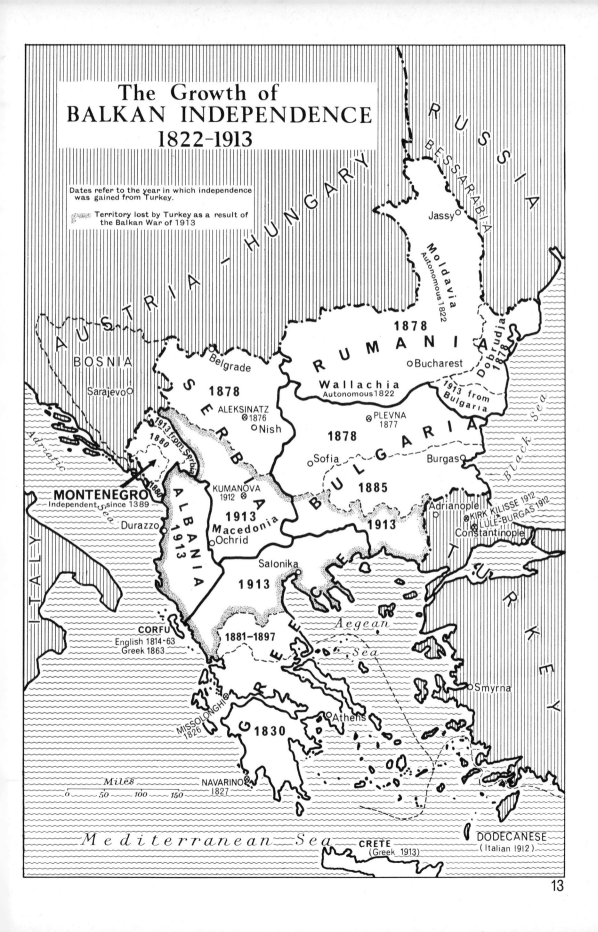

The Growth of
BALKAN INDEPENDENCE
1822-1913

Dates refer to the year in which independence
was gained from Turkey.

Territory lost by Turkey as a result of
the Balkan War of 1913

RUSSIA

AUSTRIA - HUNGARY

BESSARABIA

Jassy○

Moldavia
Autonomous 1822

BOSNIA

Belgrade○

1878

RUMANIA

○Bucharest

Dobrudia
1878

Sarajevo○

SERBIA

ALEKSINATZ
⊗1876
○Nish

1878

Wallachia
Autonomous 1822

1913 from
Bulgaria

⊗PLEVNA
1877

1878

1913 from Serbia

1880

1880

BULGARIA

○Sofia

Burgas○

Black Sea

MONTENEGRO
Independent since 1389

Durazzo

Adriatic Sea

ALBANIA
1913

KUMANOVA
1912 ⊗

1913
Macedonia
○Ochrid

1885

1913

Adrianople○
KIRK KILISSE 1912
⊗LULE-BURGAS 1912
Constantinople

ITALY

CORFU
English 1814-63
Greek 1863

Salonika○

GREECE

1913

1881-1897

Aegean
Sea

TURKEY

MISSOLONGHI⊗
1826

G 1830

○Athens

○Smyrna

Miles
0   50   100   150

NAVARINO⊗
1827

Mediterranean Sea

CRETE
(Greek 1913)

DODECANESE
(Italian 1912)

AFRICA and EUROPEAN EXPANSION to 1914

 Coastal regions under European control before 1880

Boundaries in 1914, with dates of annexation by the European powers.

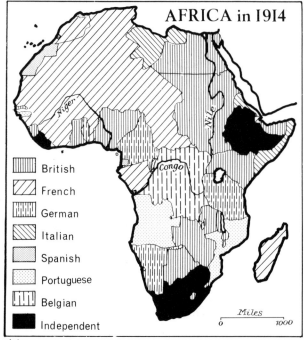

AFRICA in 1914

- British
- French
- German
- Italian
- Spanish
- Portuguese
- Belgian
- Independent

Miles
0   1000

14

Morocco FRENCH 1911

Ifni SPANISH 1860

Canary Is. SPANISH 1497

Rio De Oro SPANISH 1885

West Africa FRENCH 1909

Gambia BRITISH 1816

GUINEA PORTUGUESE 1866

Sierra Leone BRITISH 1737

Liberia Independent 1847

Ivory Coast FRENCH 1893

Gold Coast BRITISH 1874

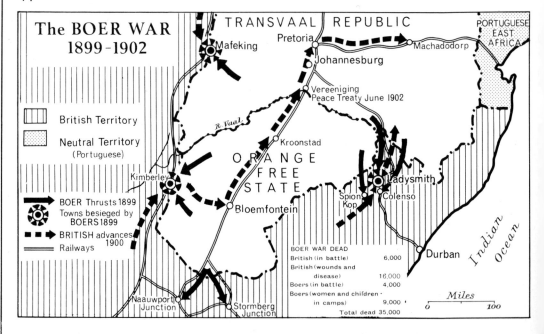

The BOER WAR 1899-1902

- British Territory
- Neutral Territory (Portuguese)
- BOER Thrusts 1899
- Towns besieged by BOERS 1899
- BRITISH advances 1900
- Railways

TRANSVAAL REPUBLIC

PORTUGUESE EAST AFRICA

Mafeking
Pretoria
Machadodorp
Johannesburg
Vereeniging
Peace Treaty June 1902
R. Vaal
Kroonstad
ORANGE FREE STATE
Kimberley
Bloemfontein
Spion Kop
Ladysmith
Colenso
Durban
Naauwport Junction
Stormberg Junction
Indian Ocean

BOER WAR DEAD	
British (in battle)	6,000
British (wounds and disease)	16,000
Boers (in battle)	4,000
Boers (women and children in camps)	9,000
Total dead 35,000	

Miles
0   100

15

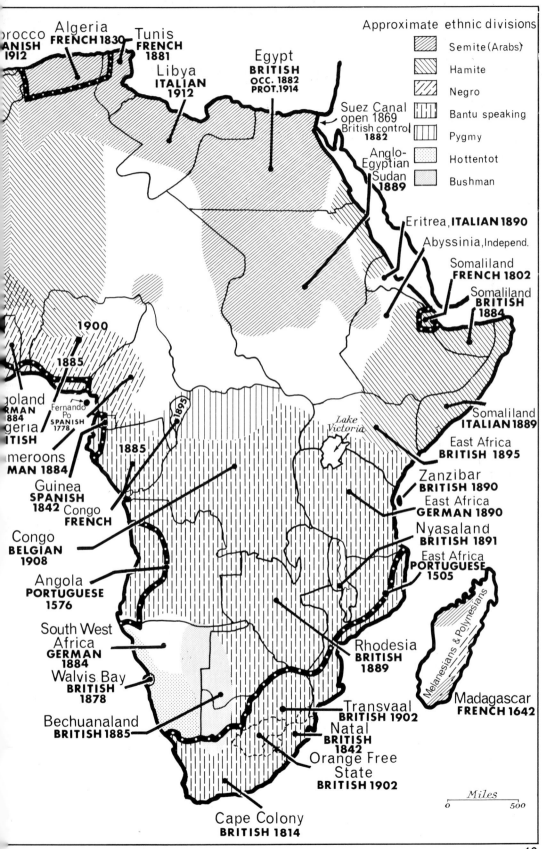

Approximate ethnic divisions

	Semite (Arabs)
	Hamite
	Negro
	Bantu speaking
	Pygmy
	Hottentot
	Bushman

Morocco **SPANISH 1912**

Algeria **FRENCH 1830**

Tunis **FRENCH 1881**

Libya **ITALIAN 1912**

Egypt **BRITISH OCC. 1882 PROT. 1914**

Suez Canal open 1869 British control **1882**

Anglo-Egyptian Sudan **1889**

Eritrea, **ITALIAN 1890**

Abyssinia, Independ.

Somaliland **FRENCH 1802**

Somaliland **BRITISH 1884**

Somaliland **ITALIAN 1889**

East Africa **BRITISH 1895**

Zanzibar **BRITISH 1890**

East Africa **GERMAN 1890**

Nyasaland **BRITISH 1891**

East Africa **PORTUGUESE 1505**

1900

1885

Togoland **GERMAN 1884**

Nigeria **BRITISH**

Fernando Po **SPANISH 1778**

Cameroons **GERMAN 1884**

Guinea **SPANISH 1842**

Congo **FRENCH**

1885

1895

Lake Victoria

Congo **BELGIAN 1908**

Angola **PORTUGUESE 1576**

South West Africa **GERMAN 1884**

Walvis Bay **BRITISH 1878**

Bechuanaland **BRITISH 1885**

Rhodesia **BRITISH 1889**

Transvaal **BRITISH 1902**

Natal **BRITISH 1842**

Orange Free State **BRITISH 1902**

Cape Colony **BRITISH 1814**

Madagascar **FRENCH 1642**

Melanesians & Polynesians

Miles
0   500

16

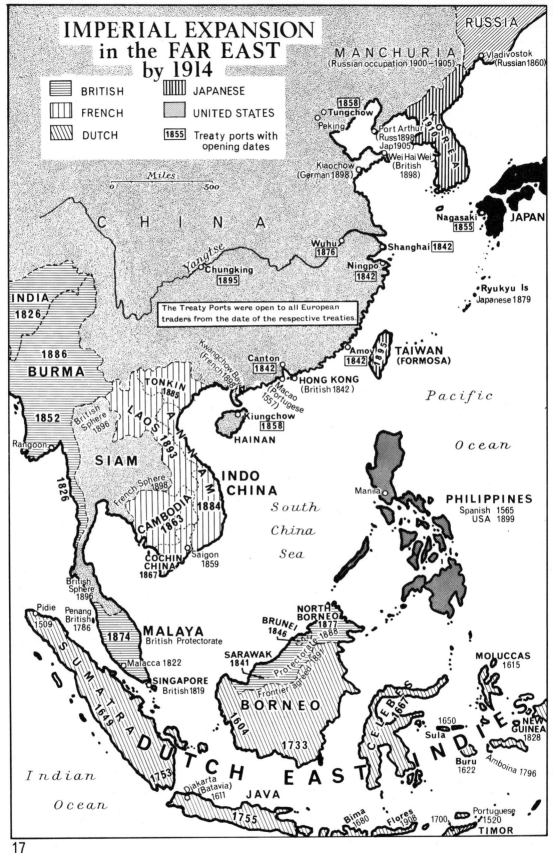

IMPERIAL EXPANSION
in the FAR EAST
by 1914

BRITISH

FRENCH

DUTCH

JAPANESE

UNITED STATES

1855 Treaty ports with opening dates

Miles
0   500

RUSSIA

MANCHURIA
(Russian occupation 1900–1905)

Vladivostok
(Russian 1860)

1858
Tungchow

Peking

Port Arthur
(Russ 1898
Jap 1905)

Kiaochow
(German 1898)

Wei Hai Wei
(British 1898)

KOREA 1910

Nagasaki
1855

JAPAN

CHINA

Yangtse

Chungking
1895

Wuhu
1876

Ningpo
1842

Shanghai 1842

Ryukyu Is
Japanese 1879

The Treaty Ports were open to all European
traders from the date of the respective treaties.

INDIA
1826

1886

BURMA

1852

Rangoon

1826

Kwangchow Bay
(French 1898)

Canton
1842

Amoy
1842

1895

TAIWAN
(FORMOSA)

Macao
(Portuguese
1557)

HONG KONG
(British 1842)

Pacific

Kiungchow
1858

HAINAN

Ocean

TONKIN
1885

LAOS 1893

ANNAM

British
Sphere
1896

SIAM

French Sphere
1898

INDO
CHINA

CAMBODIA
1863

1884

Manila

PHILIPPINES
Spanish 1565
USA 1899

South

China

Sea

COCHIN
CHINA
1867

Saigon
1859

British
Sphere
1896

Pidie
1509

Penang
British
1786

1874

MALAYA
British Protectorate

Malacca 1822

SINGAPORE
British 1819

NORTH
BORNEO
1877

BRUNEI
1846

1888

Protectorate city

SARAWAK
1841

Frontier agreed 1891

BORNEO

MOLUCCAS
1615

SUMATRA 1649

1604

1733

1753

DUTCH EAST

CELEBES 1667

Sula

1650

Buru
1622

Amboina 1796

NEW
GUINEA
1828

INDIES

Indian

Ocean

Djakarta
(Batavia)
1611

JAVA

1755

Bima
1680

Flores
1908

1700

Portuguese
1520

TIMOR

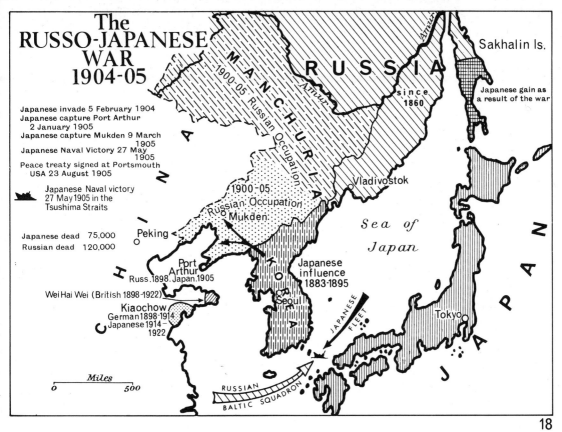

The RUSSO-JAPANESE WAR 1904-05

Japanese invade 5 February 1904
Japanese capture Port Arthur
2 January 1905
Japanese capture Mukden 9 March
1905
Japanese Naval Victory 27 May
1905
Peace treaty signed at Portsmouth
USA 23 August 1905

Japanese Naval victory
27 May 1905 in the
Tsushima Straits

Japanese dead 75,000
Russian dead 120,000

RUSSIA

MANCHURIA
1900-05 Russian Occupation

Amur

Sakhalin Is.

Japanese gain as
a result of the war

since
1860

Vladivostok

Sea of
Japan

C H I N A

1900-05
Russian Occupation

Mukden

Peking

Port
Arthur
Russ.1898. Japan.1905
Wei Hai Wei (British 1898-1922)
Kiaochow
German 1898-1914
Japanese 1914-
1922

K O R E A

Seoul

Japanese
influence
1883-1895

JAPANESE FLEET

Tokyo

J A P A N

Miles
0   500

RUSSIAN
BALTIC SQUADRON

18

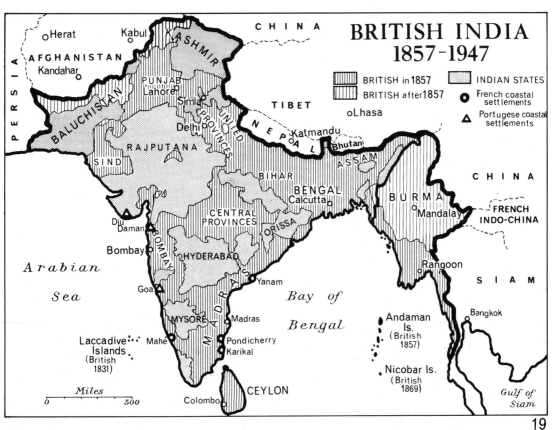

BRITISH INDIA 1857-1947

Herat
Kabul
AFGHANISTAN
Kandahar

KASHMIR

CHINA

PERSIA

BALUCHISTAN

PUNJAB
Lahore
Simla
UNITED PROVINCES
Delhi

SIND

RAJPUTANA

TIBET

oLhasa

NEPAL
Katmandu
Bhutan

ASSAM

BIHAR

BENGAL
Calcutta

CHINA

BURMA
Mandalay

FRENCH
INDO-CHINA

BRITISH in 1857   INDIAN STATES
BRITISH after 1857   ○ French coastal
                              settlements
                        △ Portugese coastal
                              settlements

Diu
Daman
Bombay
BOMBAY

CENTRAL
PROVINCES

HYDERABAD

ORISSA

Arabian
Sea

Goa

MADRAS
MYSORE
Mahé
Laccadive
Islands
(British
1831)

Yanam

Madras
Pondicherry
Karikal

Bay of
Bengal

Andaman
Is.
(British
1857)

Nicobar Is.
(British
1869)

Rangoon

SIAM

Bangkok

Gulf of
Siam

Miles
0   500

Colombo   CEYLON

19

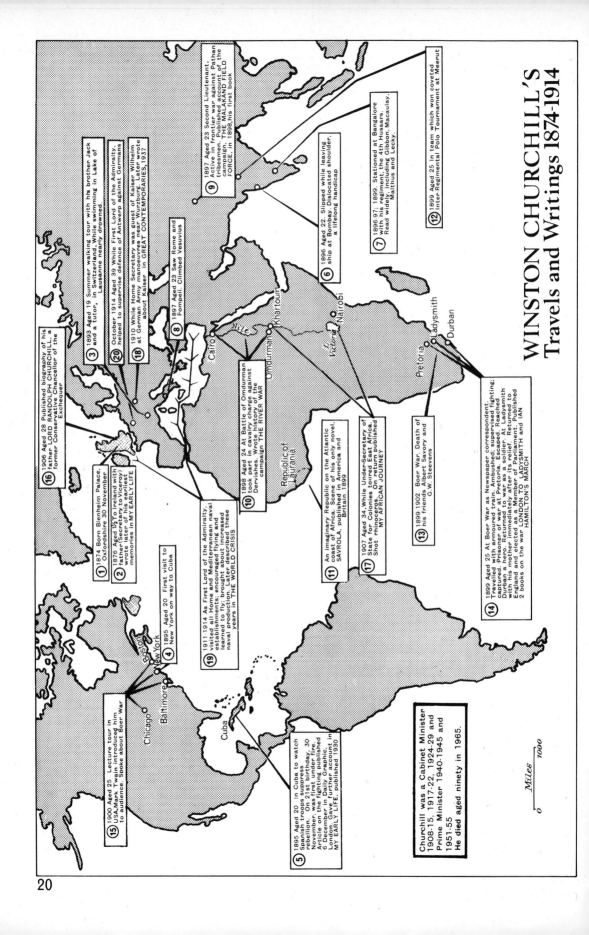

WINSTON CHURCHILL'S
Travels and Writings 1874-1914

Chicago
Baltimore
BOSTON
New York
Cuba

Cairo
Khartoum
Omdurman
Nile
L. Victoria
Nairobi
Republic of Laurania
Pretoria
Ladysmith
Durban

(1) 1874 Born Blenheim Palace, Oxfordshire 30 November

(2) 1876 Aged 1½ To Ireland with father (Secretary to Viceroy) wrote later of his earliest memories in MY EARLY LIFE

(3) 1893 Aged 19 Summer walking tour with his brother Jack and a tutor, in Switzerland. While swimming in Lake of Lausanne nearly drowned

(4) 1895 Aged 20 First visit to New York on way to Cuba

(5) 1895 Aged 20 In Cuba to watch Spanish troops suppress rebellion. On 21st birthday, 30 November, was first under fire. Article on the fighting published 6 December in Daily Graphic. London. Gave further account in MY EARLY LIFE, published 1930

(6) 1896 Aged 22. Slipped while leaving ship at Bombay. Dislocated shoulder, a lifelong handicap

(7) 1896-97; 1899. Stationed at Bangalore with his regiment, the 4th Hussars. Read widely including Gibbon, Macaulay, Malthus and Lecky.

(8) 1897 Aged 23 Saw Rome and Pompeii. Climbed Vesuvius

(9) 1897 Aged 23 Second Lieutenant. Active in frontier war against Pathan tribesmen. Published account of the campaign, THE MALAKAND FIELD FORCE, in 1898, his first book

(10) 1898 Aged 24 At Battle of Omdurman took part in cavalry charge against Dervishes. Wrote history of the campaign THE RIVER WAR

(11) An imaginary Republic on the Atlantic coast of Africa. Scene of his only novel, SAVROLA, published in America and Britain 1899

(12) 1899 Aged 25 In team which won coveted Inter-Regimental Polo Tournament at Meerut

(13) 1899-1902. Boer War. Death of his friends Albert Savory and G.W. Steevens

(14) 1899 Aged 25 At Boer War as Newspaper correspondent. Travelled with armoured train. Ambushed; supervised fighting; captured. Prisoner of war at Pretoria. Escaped. Reached Durban a hero. Returned to war as a soldier. At Ladysmith with his mother immediately after its relief. Returned to England and elected as a Member of Parliament. Published 2 books on the war LONDON TO LADYSMITH and IAN HAMILTON'S MARCH

(15) 1900 Aged 25 Lecture tour in USA.Mark Twain introduced him to audience. Spoke about Boer War

(16) 1906 Aged 28 Published biography of his father LORD RANDOLPH CHURCHILL, a former Conservative Chancellor of the Exchequer

(17) 1907 Aged 34, While Under-Secretary of State for Colonies toured East Africa. Shot rhinoceros. On return published MY AFRICAN JOURNEY

(18) 1910 While Home Secretary was guest of Kaiser Wilhelm at German Army manoeuvres near Wurzburg. Later wrote about Kaiser in GREAT CONTEMPORARIES, 1937

(19) 1911-1914 As First Lord of the Admiralty, visited all Home and Mediterranean naval establishments; encouraged flying and learned to fly; brought about increased naval production. Later described these years in THE WORLD CRISIS

(20) October 1914 Aged 39 While First Lord of the Admiralty, helped to supervise defence of Antwerp against Germans

Churchill was a Cabinet Minister 1908-15, 1917-22, 1924-29 and Prime Minister 1940-1945 and 1951-55
He died aged ninety in 1965.

Miles
0   1000

PANAMA

Canal Zone
USA 1903
to 1939

Caracas

VENEZUELA
War against Spain
1811-1821
Joined Columbia
1821-30
Then
Independ.

TRINIDAD
British
Independent 1962

BRITISH 1803
Independent 1966
Georgetown

DUTCH 1816
Paramaribo

FRENCH 1818
Cayenne

Atlantic

Ocean

Bogota

COLOMBIA
War against Spain
1811-1821.
Civil War 1831-1861

GUIANA

Quito

Secession of
Panama 1903

ECUADOR
Joined Colombia
1822
Independ.
1830

1942   1934

Amazon

Belem

B R A Z I L

Revolution against Portuguese rule 1820
Independent Empire 1822
War against Paraguay 1865-1870
Emancipation of 700,000 slaves 1888
Republic 1889

PERU
Independent
from Spain 1821

1903   1867

Lima

War against Spain
1864-1866

Bahia

La Paz

BOLIVIA
War against Spain 1809-1825
Independent 1825
War against Chile
1879-1883

Brasilia

1929

CHACO
1938   1870

Antofagasta

1884

PARAGUAY
Independent
from Spain 1811
Asuncion

1870

Rio de Janeiro

• **SAN FELIX**
Chile

1874

1874

Pacific

ARGENTINA
Independent from Spain 1810

War against Uruguay
1843-1851

War against Paraguay
1865-1870

URUGUAY
War against Portugal 1810-1830
Montevideo besieged by Argentina
1843-1851

Atlantic

Valparaiso
Santiago

**JUAN
FERNANDEZ**
Chile

CHILE
Civil War
1810-18

Buenos
Aires

Montevideo

Ocean

Ocean
Independent
from Spain
1818

PATAGONIA
1881

1902

Miles
0   500

SOUTH AMERICA
since 1800

FALKLAND
ISLANDS
British 1833
Claimed by Argentina

1881   Territory obtained after
Independence. with date.

21

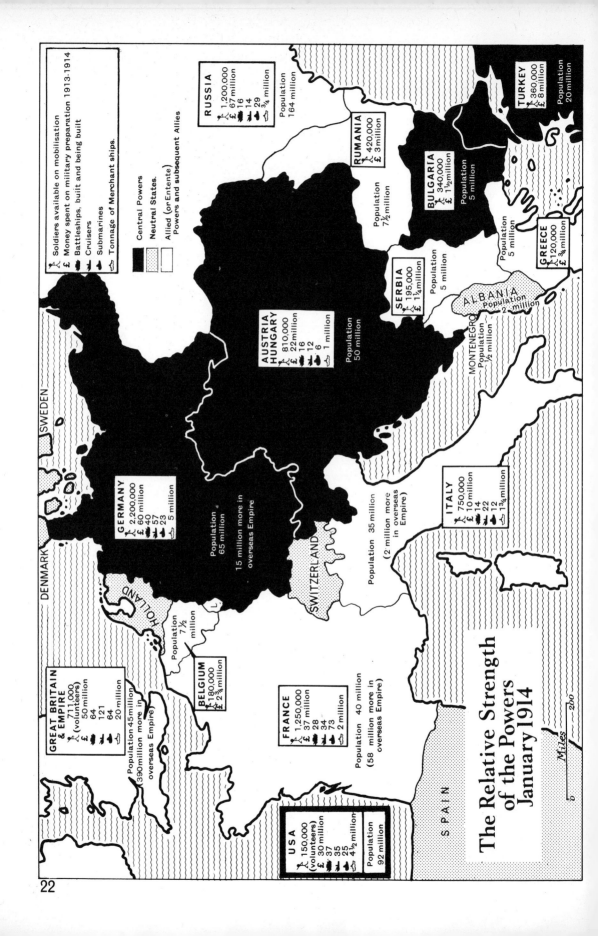

The Relative Strength of the Powers January 1914

Key:
- 👤 Soldiers available on mobilisation
- £ Money spent on military preparation 1913-1914
- Battleships, built and being built
- Cruisers
- Submarines
- Tonnage of Merchant ships.

Central Powers
Neutral States.
Allied (or Entente) Powers and subsequent Allies

GREAT BRITAIN & EMPIRE
- 👤 711,000 (volunteers)
- £ 50 million
- 64
- 121
- 64
- 20 million

Population 45 million (390 million more in overseas Empire)

USA
- 👤 150,000 (volunteers)
- £ 30 million
- 37
- 35
- 25
- 4½ million

Population 92 million

FRANCE
- 👤 1,250,000
- £ 37 million
- 28
- 34
- 73
- 2 million

Population 40 million (58 million more in overseas Empire)

BELGIUM
- 👤 180,000
- £ 2¾ million

Population 7½ million

GERMANY
- 👤 2,200,000
- £ 60 million
- 40
- 57
- 23
- 5 million

Population 65 million 15 million more in overseas Empire

AUSTRIA HUNGARY
- 👤 810,000
- £ 22 million
- 16
- 12
- 6
- 1 million

Population 50 million

ITALY
- 👤 750,000
- £ 10 million
- 14
- 22
- 12
- 1¼ million

Population 35 million (2 million more in overseas Empire)

RUSSIA
- 👤 1,200,000
- £ 67 million
- 16
- 14
- 29
- ¾ million

Population 164 million

RUMANIA
- 👤 420,000
- £ 3 million

Population 7½ million

BULGARIA
- 👤 340,000
- £ 1½ million

Population 5 million

SERBIA
- 👤 195,000
- £ 1¼ million

Population 5 million

TURKEY
- 👤 360,000
- £ 8 million

Population 20 million

GREECE
- 👤 120,000
- £ ¾ million

Population 5 million

ALBANIA Population 2 million

MONTENEGRO Population ½ million

SWEDEN

DENMARK

HOLLAND

SWITZERLAND

SPAIN

Miles
0 — 200

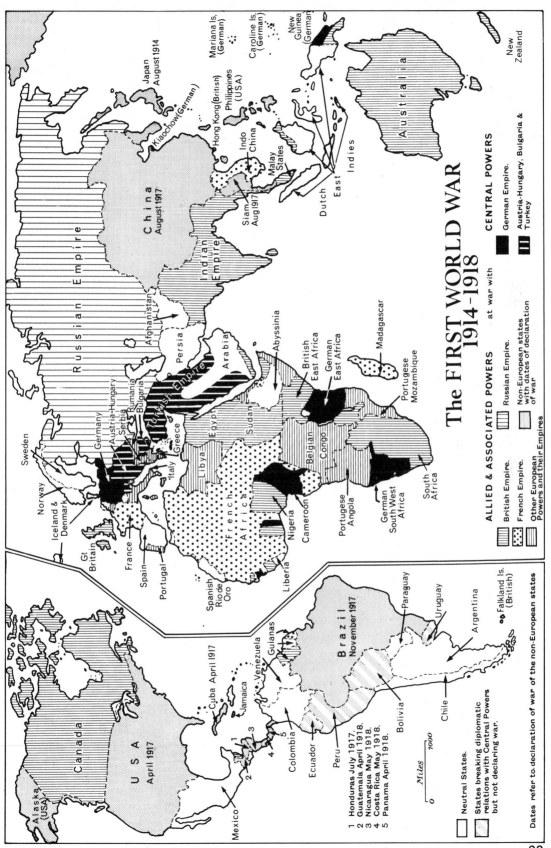

The FIRST WORLD WAR 1914-1918

—at war with

ALLIED & ASSOCIATED POWERS

British Empire.

French Empire.

Russian Empire.

Non-European states with dates of declaration of war.

Other European Powers and their Empires

CENTRAL POWERS

German Empire.

Austria-Hungary, Bulgaria & Turkey

Mariana Is. (German)

Caroline Is. (German)

New Guinea (German)

New Zealand

Japan August 1914

Kiaochow (German)

Hong Kong (British)

Philippines (USA)

Indo China

Malay States

Siam Aug 1917

Dutch East Indies

Australia

China August 1917

Indian Empire

Russian Empire

Afghanistan

Persia

Turkish Empire

Arabia

Abyssinia

British East Africa

German East Africa

Madagascar

Portugese Mozambique

Egypt

Sudan

Sweden

Norway

Iceland & Denmark

Germany

Austria-Hungary

Serbia

Bulgaria

Rumania

Italy

Greece

Libya

French Africa

Nigeria

Cameroon

Portugese Angola

German South West Africa

South Africa

Belgian Congo

Gt Britain

France

Spain

Portugal

Spanish Rio de Oro

Liberia

Alaska (USA)

Canada

USA April 1917

Mexico

Cuba April 1917

Jamaica

Honduras July 1917.

Colombia

Ecuador

Peru

Venezuela

Guianas

Brazil November 1917

Paraguay

Uruguay

Argentina

Bolivia

Chile

Falkland Is. (British)

1 Honduras July 1917.
2 Guatemala April 1918.
3 Nicaragua May 1918.
4 Costa Rica May 1918.
5 Panama April 1918.

Miles
0   1000

Neutral States.

States breaking diplomatic relations with Central Powers but not declaring war.

Dates refer to declaration of war of the non-European states

23

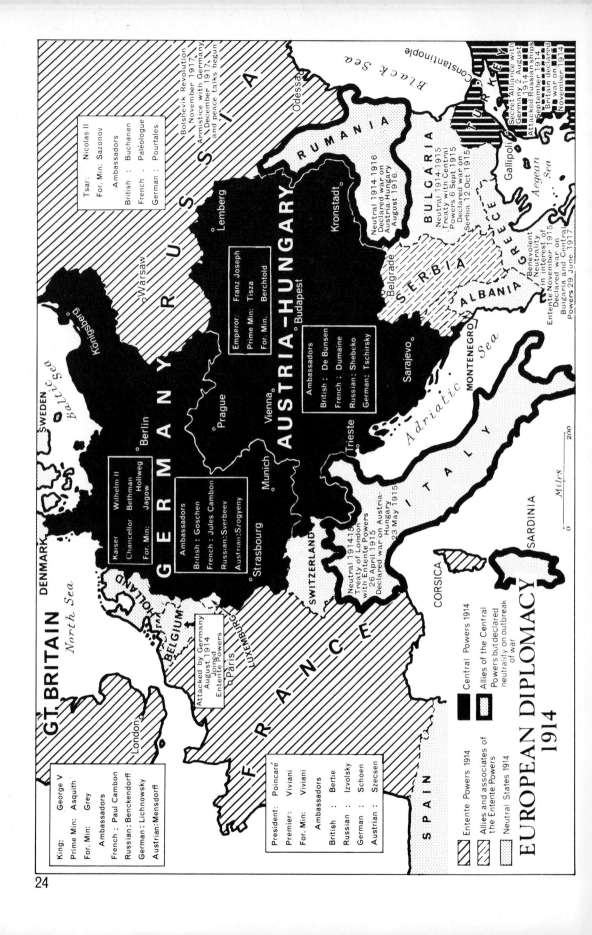

EUROPEAN DIPLOMACY
1914

Entente Powers 1914

Allies and associates of
the Entente Powers

Neutral States 1914

Central Powers 1914

Allies of the Central
Powers but declared
neutrality on outbreak
of war

GT BRITAIN

King: George V
Prime Min: Asquith
For. Min: Grey
Ambassadors
French : Paul Cambon
Russian: Benckendorff
German : Lichnowsky
Austrian: Mensdorff

FRANCE

President: Poincaré
Premier: Viviani
For. Min: Viviani
Ambassadors
British : Bertie
Russian : Izvolsky
German : Schoen
Austrian : Szecsen

GERMANY

Kaiser Wilhelm II
Chancellor Bethman Hollweg
For. Min: Jagow
Ambassadors
British : Goschen
French : Jules Cambon
Russian:Sverbeev
Austrian:Szogyeny

AUSTRIA–HUNGARY

Emperor: Franz Joseph
Prime Min: Tisza
For. Min: Berchtold
Ambassadors
British : De Bunsen
French : Dumaine
Russian: Shebeko
German: Tschirsky

RUSSIA

Tsar: Nicolas II
For. Min: Sazonov
Ambassadors
British : Buchanan
French : Paléologue
German : Pourtales

Bolshevik Revolution
November 1917
Armistice with Germany
December 1917,
and peace talks begun

RUMANIA
Neutral 1914-1916
Declared war on
Austria-Hungary
August 1916

BULGARIA
Neutral 1914-1915
Treaty with Central
Powers 6 Sept 1915
Declared war on
Serbia 12 Oct 1915

SERBIA

ALBANIA

GREECE
Benevolent
Neutrality
in interest of
Entente November 1915
Declared war on
Bulgaria and Central
Powers 29 June 1917

MONTENEGRO

TURKEY
Secret Alliance with
Germany 2 August
1914
Attacked Russian ships
September 1914
Britain declared
war on
November 1914

Gallipoli

Constantinople

ITALY
Neutral 1914-15
Treaty of London
with Entente Powers
26 April 1915
Declared war on Austria-
Hungary
23 May 1915

BELGIUM
Attacked by Germany
August 1914
Joined
Entente Powers

SWEDEN

DENMARK

HOLLAND

LUXEMBURG

SWITZERLAND

SPAIN

SARDINIA

CORSICA

Black Sea

Odessa

Lemberg

Kronstadt

Warsaw

Königsberg

Berlin

Prague

Budapest

Vienna

Munich

Sarajevo

Belgrade

Trieste

Strasbourg

Paris

London

Baltic Sea

North Sea

Adriatic Sea

Aegean Sea

Miles
0   200

24

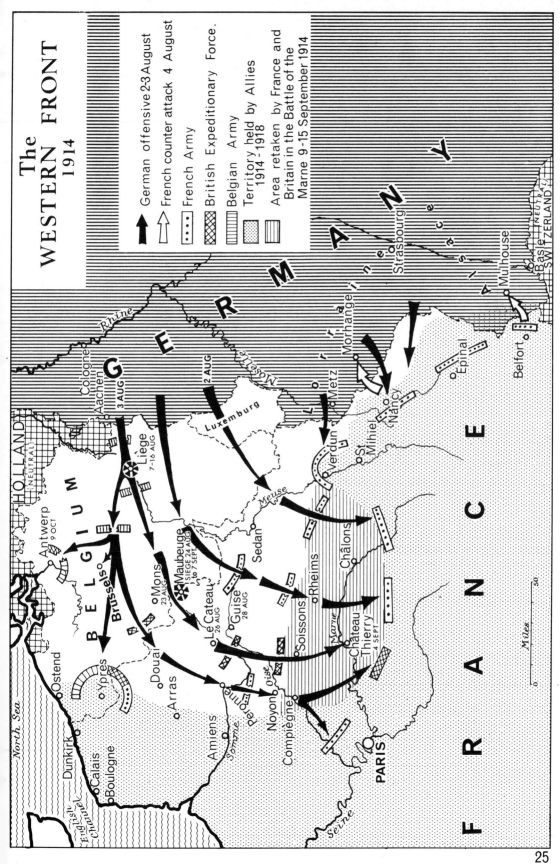

The
WESTERN FRONT
1914

German offensive 23 August
French counter attack 4 August

French Army
British Expeditionary Force.
Belgian Army
Territory held by Allies
1914 - 1918
Area retaken by France and
Britain in the Battle of the
Marne 9-15 September 1914

North Sea

GERMANY

HOLLAND (NEUTRAL)

English Channel

Rhine

Cologne
Aachen
2 AUG
3 AUG

Moselle

Rhine

BELGIUM

Liège
7-16 AUG

Luxemburg

Antwerp
9 OCT

Brussels

Mons
23 AUG

Maubeuge
SIEGE 24 AUG
to 7 SEPT

Le Cateau
26 AUG

Guise
28 AUG

Sedan

Meuse

Lorraine

Metz
Verdun
St.
Mihiel

Morhange

Nancy

Strasbourg

Alsace

Ostend

Ypres

Douai

Arras

Amiens

Somme

Scarpe

Noyon
Compiègne

Oise

Soissons

Rheims

Châlons

Château
Thierry
4 SEPT

Marne

Belfort

Epinal

SWITZERLAND
(NEUTRAL)

Basle

Mulhouse

Dunkirk
Calais
Boulogne

PARIS

F   R   A   N   C   E

Seine

Miles
0   50

25

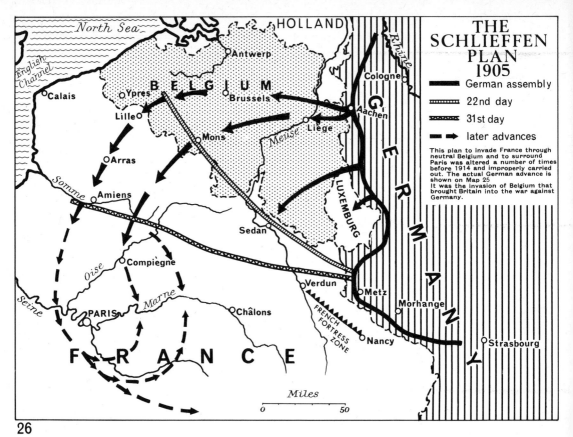

THE
SCHLIEFFEN
PLAN
1905

━━━ German assembly
┄┄┄ 22nd day
∿∿∿ 31st day
┅► later advances

This plan to invade France through
neutral Belgium and to surround
Paris was altered a number of times
before 1914 and improperly carried
out. The actual German advance is
shown on Map 25
It was the invasion of Belgium that
brought Britain into the war against
Germany.

North Sea

English Channel

HOLLAND

Antwerp

B E L G I U M

Calais

Ypres
Lille

Brussels

Cologne

G Aachen

Mons
Liège

Meuse

Rhine

LUXEMBURG

Arras

Somme

Amiens

Sedan

Oise

Compiègne

Marne

Seine

PARIS

Châlons

Verdun

Metz

Morhange

FRENCH
FORTRESS
ZONE

Nancy

G E R M A N Y

Strasbourg

F R A N C E

Miles

0   50

26

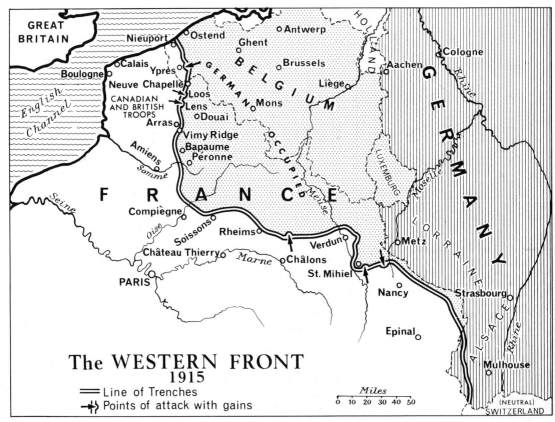

GREAT
BRITAIN

North Sea

Nieuport
Ostend

Antwerp

Ghent

HOLLAND

Calais
Boulogne

Ypres

G
E
R
M
A
N

B E L G I U M

Brussels

Aachen

Cologne

Neuve Chapelle

Liège

Rhine

CANADIAN
AND BRITISH
TROOPS

Loos
Lens
Douai

Mons

English Channel

Arras

Vimy Ridge
Bapaume
Peronne

O
C
C
U
P
I
E
D

Meuse

LUXEMBURG

Moselle

Amiens

Somme

F R A N C E

G
E
R
M
A
N
Y

Seine

Compiègne

Oise

Soissons

Rheims

Château Thierry

Marne

Châlons

Verdun

Metz

L
O
R
R
A
I
N
E

PARIS

St. Mihiel

Nancy

Strasbourg

A
L
S
A
C
E

Rhine

Epinal

Mulhouse

(NEUTRAL)
SWITZERLAND

The WESTERN FRONT
1915

═══ Line of Trenches
┅► Points of attack with gains

Miles
0 10 20 30 40 50

27

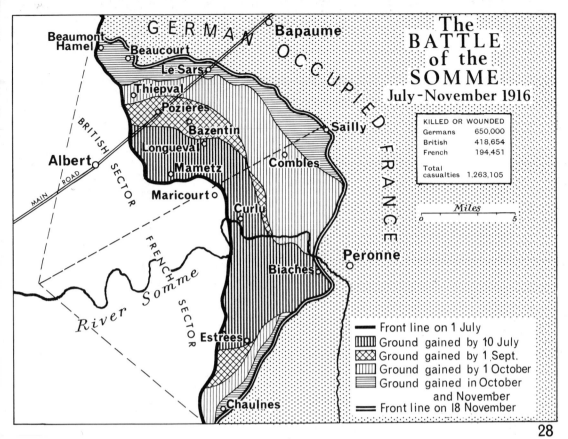

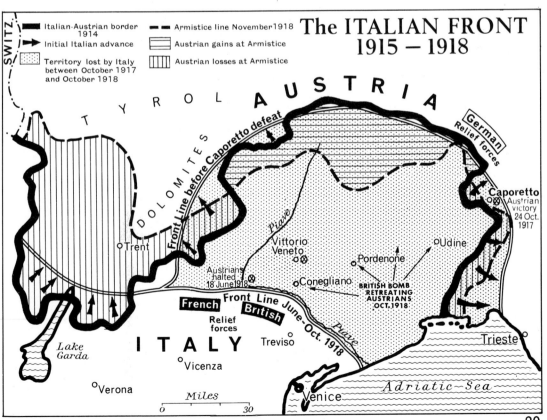

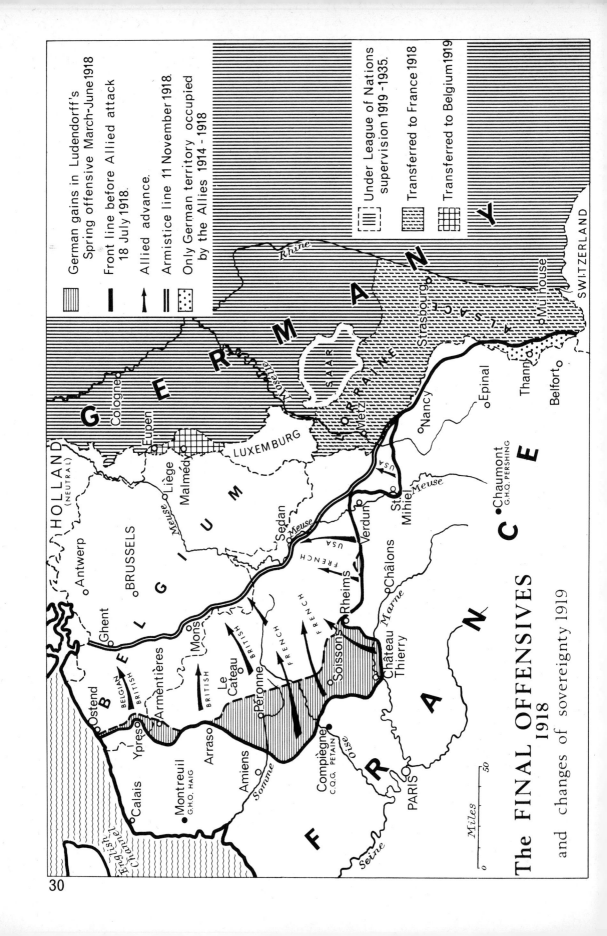

Legend

- German gains in Ludendorff's Spring offensive March-June 1918
- Front line before Allied attack 18 July 1918.
- Allied advance.
- Armistice line 11 November 1918.
- Only German territory occupied by the Allies 1914 - 1918
- Under League of Nations supervision 1919 -1935.
- Transferred to France 1918
- Transferred to Belgium 1919

Map Labels

SWITZERLAND

GERMANY

Rhine

Mulhouse
Strasbourg
ALSACE
Thann
Belfort

SAAR
Metz
LORRAINE
Nancy
Epinal

Cologne
Eupen
Meuse

Chaumont
G.H.Q. PERSHING

HOLLAND (NEUTRAL)

Liège
Malmédy
Sedan
Meuse
Verdun
St. Mihiel
Meuse
USA
Châlons
Marne

LUXEMBURG

Antwerp
BRUSSELS
BELGIUM

USA
FRENCH
Rheims
FRENCH
FRENCH
Château Thierry

Ghent
Mons
Armentières
BELGIAN
BRITISH
Le Cateau
BRITISH
Péronne
Soissons

Ostend
Ypres
Arras
BRITISH
Amiens
Somme
Compiègne
C.Q.G. PETAIN

Calais
Montreuil
G.H.Q. HAIG
Oise

English Channel

FRANCE
PARIS
Seine
Marne

Miles
0   50

The FINAL OFFENSIVES 1918
and changes of sovereignty 1919

The EASTERN FRONT
August 1914 – January 1915

Baltic Sea

Königsberg

Danzig

Gumbinnen
(Russian victory
20 Aug)

Elbing

Gerdauen

Bischofstein

P R U S S I A

Masurian Lakes

Tannenberg

Vistula

Bug

WARSAW

Brest Litovsk

Pripet

Pinsk

Marshes

Lodz

R U S S I A

Lublin

Krasnik

Komarov

Vistula

San

Rava Russkaya

Cracow

Tarnow

Przemysl

Lemberg

Gorlice

C A R P A T H I A N   M O U N T A I N S

A U S T R I A

Stanislau

Dniester

	Russian gains to August 25
	German retreat and counterattack
	Russian defeat 27 August and attempted line of retreat
	German attack 28 September
	LODZ: German armies trapped, beseiged by Russians, but broke out Lodz captured 6 December

	Austrian advance and retreat
	Russian advance
	Russian losses to Germany 1914
	Austrian losses to Russia 1914
	Final Winter line 1914-1915.

Miles

0   50   100

The
EASTERN FRONT
1915

	Area gained by Germany and Austria Jan–July
	Area gained by Germany and Austria Aug–Sept
➤	October offensive
	Serbian Army – November
➡	Final Serbian withdrawal
⋯▷	French Expeditionary Force
⊞▷	British landings April & August

Miles
0   100   200

German forces
Austrian forces

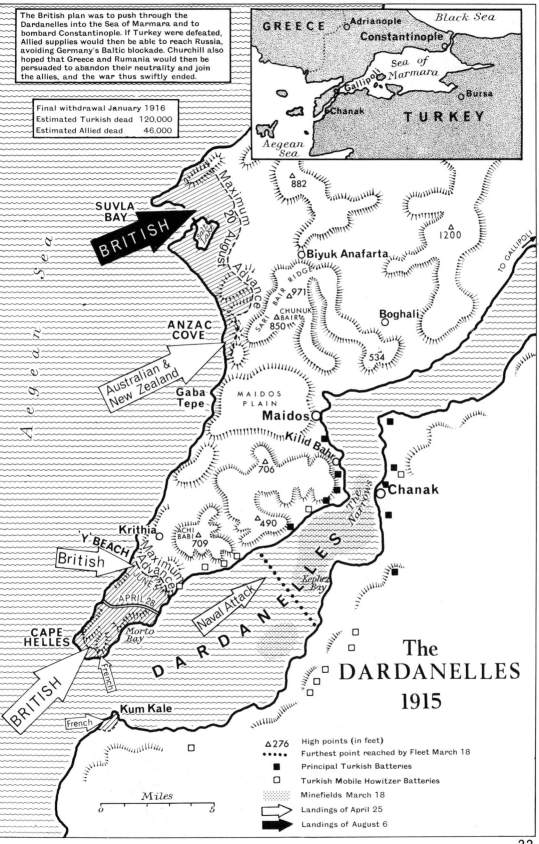

The British plan was to push through the Dardanelles into the Sea of Marmara and to bombard Constantinople. If Turkey were defeated, Allied supplies would then be able to reach Russia, avoiding Germany's Baltic blockade. Churchill also hoped that Greece and Rumania would then be persuaded to abandon their neutrality and join the allies, and the war thus swiftly ended.

Final withdrawal January 1916
Estimated Turkish dead   120,000
Estimated Allied dead   46,000

GREECE
Adrianople
Black Sea
Constantinople
Sea of Marmara
Gallipoli
Chanak
Bursa
TURKEY
Aegean Sea

△ 882
△ 1200

TO GALLIPOLI

SUVLA BAY
BRITISH
Salt Lake

Biyuk Anafarta
SARI BAIR RIDGE △ 971
CHUNUK △ BAIR
850
Boghali
△ 534

ANZAC COVE
Australian & New Zealand

Gaba Tepe

MAIDOS PLAIN
Maidos
Kilid Bahr
△ 706

The Narrows
Chanak

△ 490

Krithia
ACHI BABI △
709

'Y' BEACH
British
Maximum Advance JUNE 5
APRIL 28

Kephez Bay

Naval Attack

CAPE HELLES
Morto Bay

BRITISH
French

DARDANELLES

The
DARDANELLES
1915

Kum Kale
French

Miles
0   5

△276   High points (in feet)
•••••   Furthest point reached by Fleet March 18
■   Principal Turkish Batteries
□   Turkish Mobile Howitzer Batteries
░░   Minefields March 18
⇨   Landings of April 25
➡   Landings of August 6

33

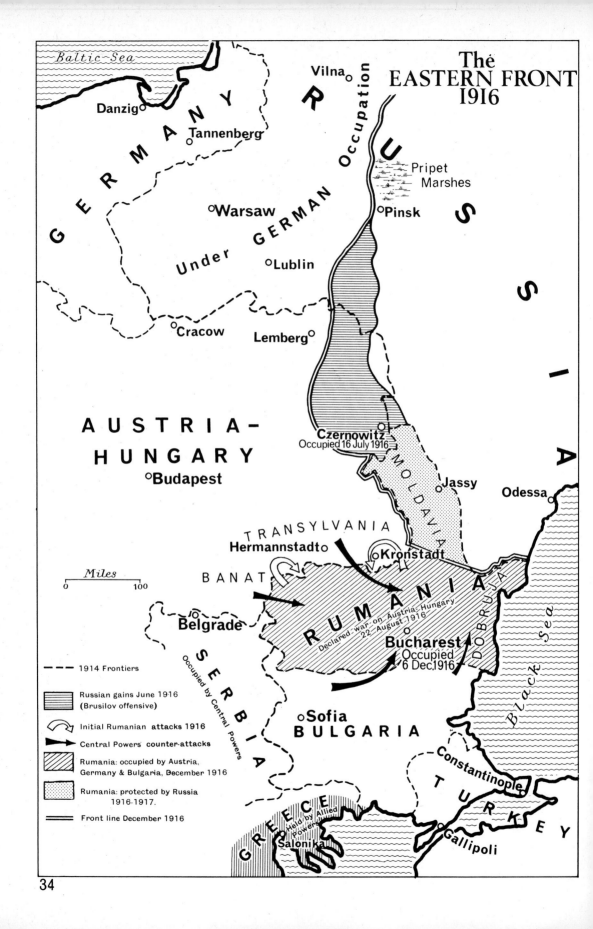

Baltic Sea

The **EASTERN FRONT 1916**

G E R M A N Y

Danzig

Tannenberg

R U S S I A

Vilna

Occupation

Pripet Marshes

Warsaw

Under GERMAN

Pinsk

Lublin

Cracow

Lemberg

A U S T R I A - H U N G A R Y

Budapest

Czernowitz
Occupied 16 July 1916

M O L D A V I A

Jassy

Odessa

T R A N S Y L V A N I A

Hermannstadt

Kronstadt

B A N A T

R U M A N I A

Declared war on Austria-Hungary 22 August 1916

D O B R U J A

Belgrade

Bucharest
Occupied
6 Dec. 1916

Black Sea

Miles
0   100

S E R B I A

Occupied by Central Powers

Sofia
B U L G A R I A

1914 Frontiers

Russian gains June 1916
(Brusilov offensive)

Initial Rumanian attacks 1916

Central Powers counter-attacks

Rumania: occupied by Austria,
Germany & Bulgaria, December 1916

Rumania: protected by Russia
1916-1917.

Front line December 1916

Constantinople

T U R K E Y

G R E E C E

Held by Allied Powers

Salonika

Gallipoli

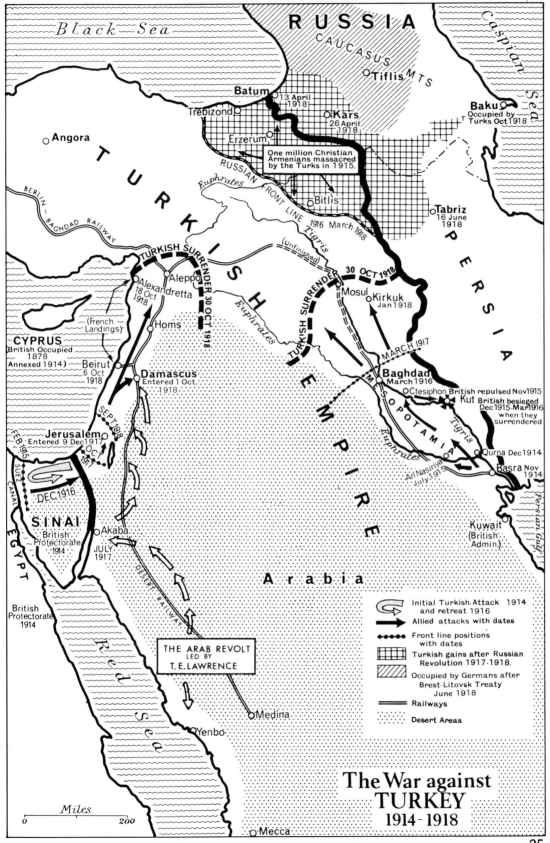

Black Sea

R U S S I A

CAUCASUS MTS

Tiflis

Batum 13 April 1918
Trebizond

o **Angora**

Kars 26 April 1918

Erzerum

One million Christian Armenians massacred by the Turks in 1915.

Euphrates

RUSSIAN FRONT LINE

1916 March 1918

Tigris

Bitlis

Tabriz 16 June 1918

Baku Occupied by Turks Oct 1918

Caspian Sea

BERLIN – BAGHDAD RAILWAY

T U R K I S H   E M P I R E

(Unfinished)

TURKISH SURRENDER 30 OCT 1918

30 OCT 1918

TURKISH SURRENDER

o **Aleppo**

Alexandretta 18 Oct 1918

(French Landings)

CYPRUS
British Occupied 1878
Annexed 1914)

o Homs

Beirut 6 Oct 1918

Damascus Entered 1 Oct. 1918

SEPT 1918

Euphrates

Mosul o

Kirkuk Jan 1918

MARCH 1917

P E R S I A

Baghdad March 1916
o Ctesiphon British repulsed Nov 1915
Kut British besieged Dec 1915-Mar 1916 when they surrendered

M E S O P O T A M I A

Tigris

Euphrates

An Nasiriya July 1915

Qurna Dec 1914

Basra Nov 1914

Jerusalem Entered 9 Dec 1917

FEB 1915

OCT 1917

SUEZ CANAL

DEC 1916

SINAI British Protectorate 1914

Akaba

JULY 1917

EGYPT

British Protectorate 1914

Red Sea

DESERT RAILWAY

A r a b i a

Kuwait (British Admin.)

Persian Gulf

THE ARAB REVOLT
LED BY
T. E. LAWRENCE

o **Medina**

o Yenbo

Initial Turkish Attack 1914 and retreat 1916

Allied attacks with dates

Front line positions with dates

Turkish gains after Russian Revolution 1917-1918.

Occupied by Germans after Brest-Litovsk Treaty June 1918

Railways

Desert Areas

Miles
0   200

The War against TURKEY 1914-1918

o Mecca

The WAR in the BALKANS
1915-1918

AUSTRIA-HUNGARY

BELGRADE
Nov. 1913

Sarajevo

MONTENEGRO

S E R B I A
300,000 Serbs
died in Typhus
Epidemic 1915

Nish
Oct 1918

Ochrid

ALBANIA

Valona

FRONT LINE

ITALIAN
DEC.1915

ITALY

CORFU

FRENCH
JAN 1916

G R E E C E

AUG.1916 – AUG.1918

Miles
0   50

RUMANIA

BUCHAREST

Danube

Rustchuk

Plevna

SOFIA

B U L G A R I A
Capitulated 29 September 1918

Adrianople

Salonika
Oct.1915

Aegean
Sea

LEMNOS

BRITISH & FRENCH
OCT 1915

Black Sea

Constantinople

T U R K E Y

Gallipoli

Chanak

DARDANELLES

1915-16

Central Powers   Occupied by Central Powers 1915-17

Allied Landings   Allied advances

36

RUSSIAN TERRITORIAL
LOSSES 1917-18

SWEDEN

Petrograd

Tallinn

Riga

The Bolshevik revolution
of November 1917 was
followed immediately by
an appeal to Germany for
peace

Miles
0   200

Moscow

Baltic Sea

GERMANY

Berlin

Vilna

Warsaw

Lodz

Minsk

Mohilev

R U S S I A

Orel

Brest Litovsk

Prague

AUSTRIA–
HUNGARY

Vienna

Czernowitz

U K R A I N E

Kiev

Dnieper

Kharkov

Don

Rostov

Jassy

Odessa

Dniester

Sea of Azov

RUMANIA

Bucharest

Black Sea

Novorossiisk

Front line at Armistice 5 December 1917

Ceded by Bolshevik Government to Germany
by the Treaty of Brest Litovsk 3 March 1917

Occupied by Germany 1918

Occupied by Austria 1918

Occupied by Rumania 1918

37

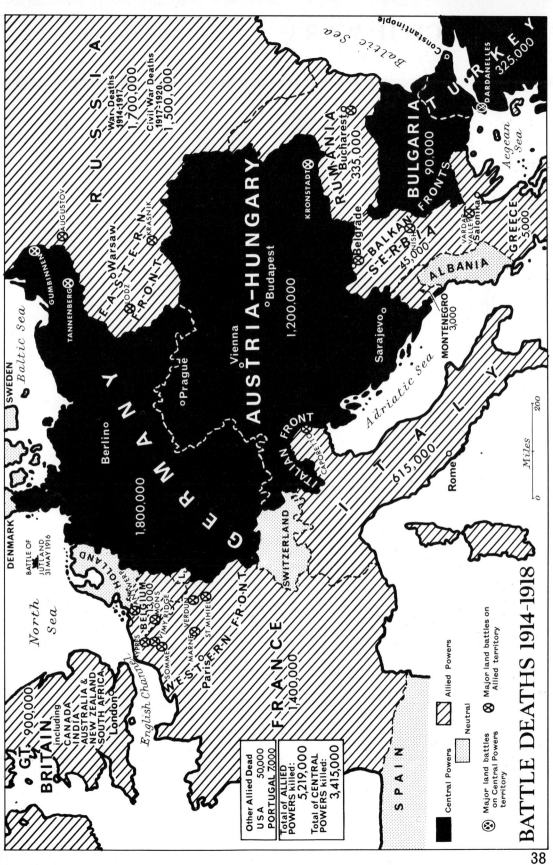

BATTLE DEATHS 1914-1918

RUSSIA
War Deaths 1914-1917
1,700,000
Civil War Deaths 1917-1920.
1,500,000

Constantinople

TURKEY
325,000
DARDANELLES

BULGARIA
90,000
FRONTS

RUMANIA
Bucharest
335,000

Balkan
Belgrade
SERBIA
NISH
45,000

GREECE
5,000
VARDAR VALLEY
Salonika

ALBANIA

MONTENEGRO
3,000

AUSTRIA-HUNGARY
Budapest
1,200,000

Vienna

Sarajevo

Prague

Berlin

GERMANY
1,800,000

ITALIAN FRONT
CAPORETTO

ITALY
615,000

Rome

EASTERN FRONT
Warsaw
LODZ
KRASNIK
AUGUSTOV
GUMBINNEN
TANNENBERG

KRONSTADT

SWEDEN

Baltic Sea

Aegean Sea

Adriatic Sea

DENMARK

BATTLE OF JUTLAND 31 MAY 1916

HOLLAND

BELGIUM 13,000

YPRES
MONS
VIMY RIDGE
SOMME
MARNE
VERDUN
ST MIHIEL

WESTERN FRONT
PARIS
FRANCE
1,400,000

SWITZERLAND

North Sea

English Channel

London

GT. BRITAIN
900,000
including
CANADA
INDIA
AUSTRALIA &
NEW ZEALAND
SOUTH AFRICA

SPAIN

Miles
0   200

Other Allied Dead	
USA	50,000
PORTUGAL	7,000

Total of ALLIED
POWERS killed:
5,219,000

Total of CENTRAL
POWERS killed:
3,415,000

Central Powers

Allied Powers

Neutral

Major land battles on
Central Powers territory

Major land battles on
Allied territory

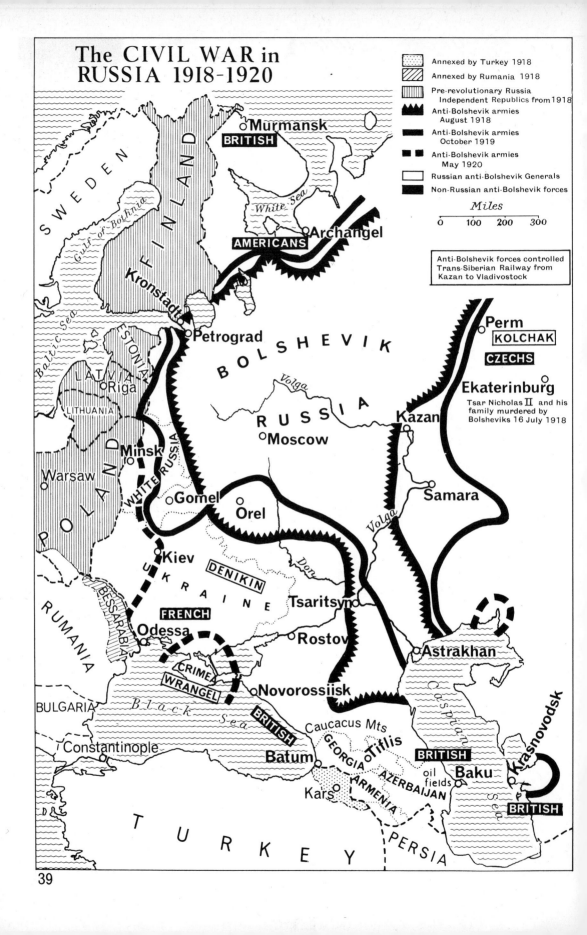

The CIVIL WAR in RUSSIA 1918-1920

Annexed by Turkey 1918

Annexed by Rumania 1918

Pre-revolutionary Russia Independent Republics from 1918

Anti-Bolshevik armies August 1918

Anti-Bolshevik armies October 1919

Anti-Bolshevik armies May 1920

Russian anti-Bolshevik Generals

Non-Russian anti-Bolshevik forces

Miles

0   100   200   300

Anti-Bolshevik forces controlled Trans-Siberian Railway from Kazan to Vladivostock

SWEDEN

FINLAND

White Sea

Murmansk

BRITISH

Archangel

AMERICANS

Gulf of Bothnia

Kronstadt

Baltic Sea

Petrograd

BOLSHEVIK

Perm

KOLCHAK

CZECHS

ESTONIA

LATVIA

Riga

LITHUANIA

RUSSIA

Volga

Ekaterinburg

Tsar Nicholas II and his family murdered by Bolsheviks 16 July 1918

Moscow

Kazan

Warsaw

Minsk

WHITE RUSSIA

Gomel

Orel

Samara

Volga

POLAND

UKRAINE

Kiev

DENIKIN

Don

RUMANIA

BESSARABIA

Odessa

FRENCH

Tsaritsyn

Rostov

Astrakhan

CRIMEA

WRANGEL

Novorossiisk

Caspian Sea

BULGARIA

Black Sea

BRITISH

Caucacus Mts

Constantinople

Batum

GEORGIA

Tiflis

AZERBAIJAN

BRITISH

oil fields

Baku

Krasnovodsk

Kars

ARMENIA

BRITISH

TURKEY

PERSIA

39

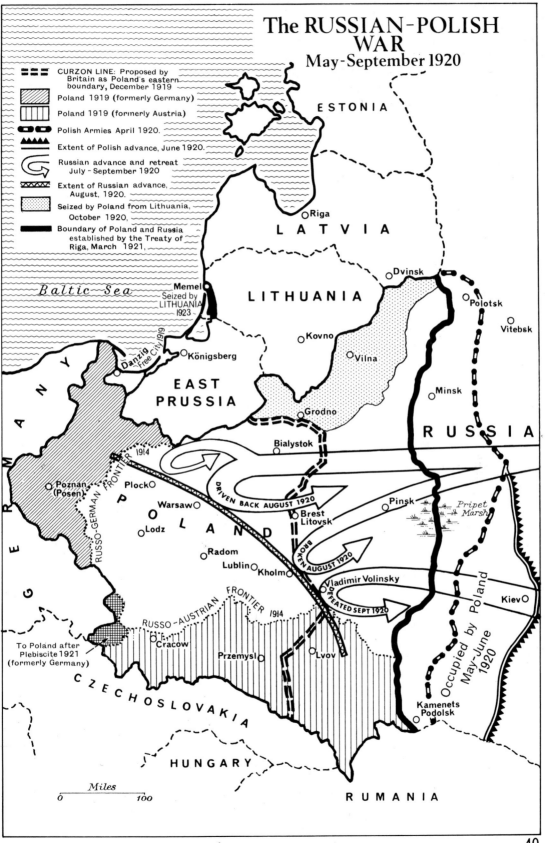

The RUSSIAN-POLISH WAR
May-September 1920

CURZON LINE: Proposed by Britain as Poland's eastern boundary, December 1919

Poland 1919 (formerly Germany)

Poland 1919 (formerly Austria)

Polish Armies April 1920.

Extent of Polish advance, June 1920.

Russian advance and retreat July-September 1920

Extent of Russian advance, August, 1920.

Seized by Poland from Lithuania, October 1920.

Boundary of Poland and Russia established by the Treaty of Riga, March 1921.

Baltic Sea

ESTONIA

LATVIA

LITHUANIA

RUSSIA

Riga

Dvinsk

Polotsk

Vitebsk

Memel
Seized by
LITHUANIA
1923

Kovno

Vilna

Minsk

Danzig
Free City 1919

Königsberg

EAST
PRUSSIA

Grodno

Bialystok

G E R M A N Y

Poznan
(Posen)

Plock

RUSSO-GERMAN FRONTIER 1914

P
O
L
A
N
D

Warsaw

Lodz

DRIVEN BACK AUGUST 1920

Pinsk

Pripet Marsh

Brest
Litovsk

BROKEN AUGUST 1920

Radom

Lublin

Kholm

Vladimir Volinsky

DEFEATED SEPT 1920

Kiev

Occupied by Poland May-June 1920

To Poland after
Plebiscite 1921
(formerly Germany)

RUSSO-AUSTRIAN FRONTIER 1914

Cracow

Przemysl

Lvov

Kamenets
Podolsk

C Z E C H O S L O V A K I A

H U N G A R Y

R U M A N I A

Miles
0   100

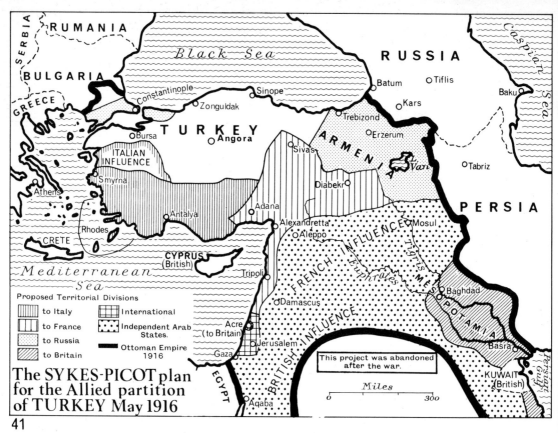

Proposed Territorial Divisions

||||||| to Italy	⊞ International
to France	⠿ Independent Arab States.
to Russia	▬ Ottoman Empire 1916
to Britain	

This project was abandoned after the war.

Miles
0   300

The SYKES-PICOT plan for the Allied partition of TURKEY May 1916

41

Greek Minority areas 1918

Awarded to Greece at Treaty of Sevres 1919

British controlled zone of the straits 1920-22.

Turkish advances, 1922.

Transfer of populations after 1922 :—

➤ Greeks 1,377,000
⇨ Turks 410,000
-➤ Bulgarians.....250,000

—·—·Final western frontier of Turkey

Miles
0   200

The War between GREECE & TURKEY 1922

42

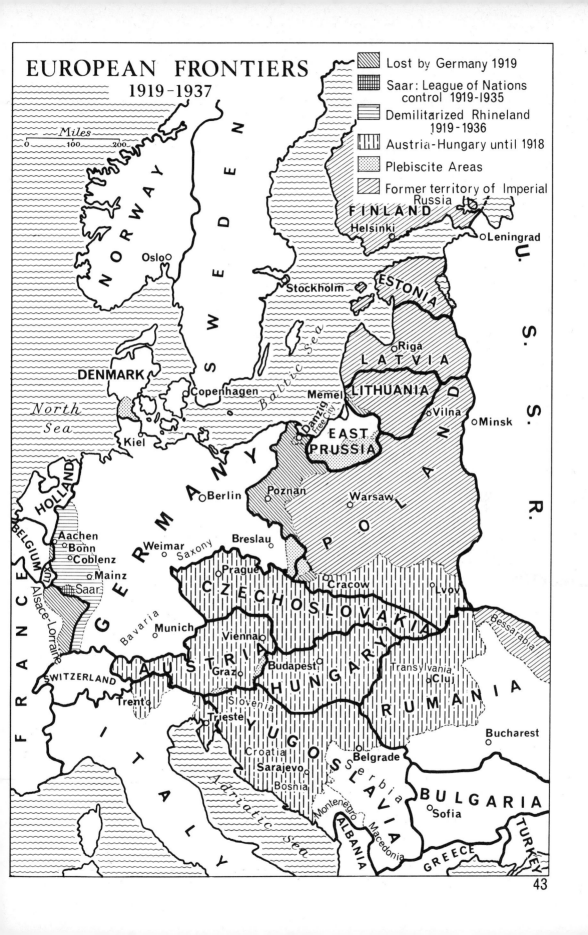

EUROPEAN FRONTIERS
1919–1937

Miles
0   100   200

Lost by Germany 1919
Saar: League of Nations control 1919–1935
Demilitarized Rhineland 1919–1936
Austria-Hungary until 1918
Plebiscite Areas
Former territory of Imperial Russia

NORWAY

SWEDEN

FINLAND
Helsinki
Leningrad

Oslo

Stockholm

ESTONIA

DENMARK

LATVIA
Riga

Copenhagen
Memel
LITHUANIA
Vilna
Minsk

North Sea

Baltic Sea

Kiel

Danzig Free City

EAST PRUSSIA

Berlin
Poznan
Warsaw

POLAND

HOLLAND
BELGIUM
Aachen
Bonn
Coblenz
Mainz
Saar
Alsace-Lorraine
Weimar
Saxony
Breslau

GERMANY

Cracow
Lvov

Prague

CZECHOSLOVAKIA

Bessarabia

FRANCE

SWITZERLAND

Bavaria
Munich

Vienna
Graz

AUSTRIA

Budapest

HUNGARY

Transylvania
Cluj

RUMANIA

Trent

Slovenia
Trieste

Croatia

Sarajevo
Bosnia

YUGOSLAVIA

Belgrade

Serbia

Bucharest

ITALY

Adriatic Sea

Montenegro
Macedonia

ALBANIA

BULGARIA
Sofia

GREECE

TURKEY

U. S. S. R.

43

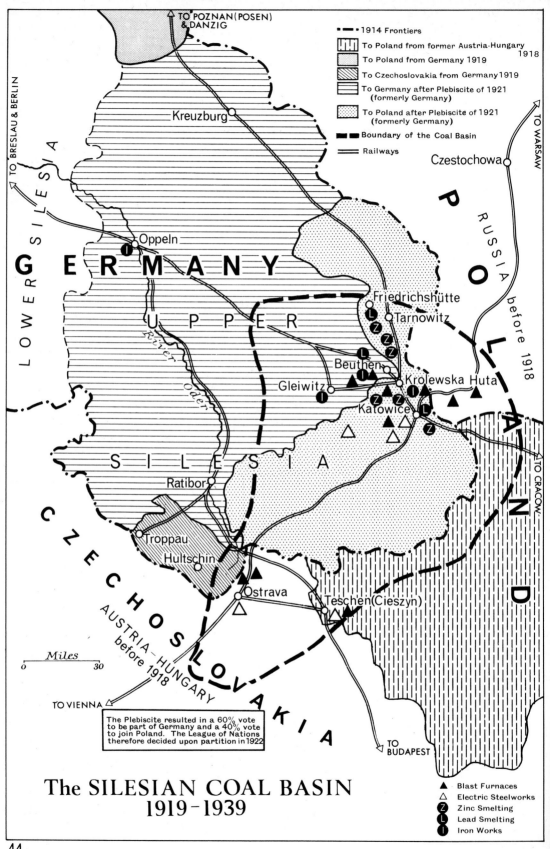

TO POZNAN (POSEN) & DANZIG

TO BRESLAU & BERLIN

LOWER SILESIA

Kreuzburg

TO WARSAW

POLAND

Czestochowa

RUSSIA before 1918

GERMANY

Oppeln

UPPER

River Oder

Friedrichshütte

L
Z

Tarnowitz

Z
Z

Beuthen

L

Krolewska Huta

Gleiwitz

I

Z
Z
I
L

Katowice

Z

SILESIA

Ratibor

Troppau

Hultschin

CZECHOSLOVAKIA

TO CRACOW

Ostrava

Teschen (Cieszyn)

AUSTRIA-HUNGARY before 1918

TO VIENNA

Miles
0   30

The Plebiscite resulted in a 60% vote
to be part of Germany and a 40% vote
to join Poland. The League of Nations
therefore decided upon partition in 1922

TO BUDAPEST

**The SILESIAN COAL BASIN
1919–1939**

Legend:
- - - · 1914 Frontiers
To Poland from former Austria-Hungary 1918
To Poland from Germany 1919
To Czechoslovakia from Germany 1919
To Germany after Plebiscite of 1921 (formerly Germany)
To Poland after Plebiscite of 1921 (formerly Germany)
━ ━ ━ Boundary of the Coal Basin
══ Railways

▲ Blast Furnaces
△ Electric Steelworks
Ⓩ Zinc Smelting
Ⓛ Lead Smelting
Ⓘ Iron Works

GERMANY

P O L A N D

C Z E C H O S L O V A K I A

Prague
Cracow
Lvov
Brno
Chust
Munich
Linz
Bratislava
Satmar
Vienna
Czernowitz
Innsbruck

A U S T R I A
Budapest
H U N G A R Y
R U M A N I A

I T A L Y
Trent
Szeged
Ljubljana
Zagreb
Temisoara
Trieste
Y U G O S L A V I A
Kikinda
Fiume
Belgrade

Miles
0   100

Sarajevo

The Disruption of Rail Communications in Central Europe, 1919.

Following the break-up of the Habsburg Empire and establishment of customs and tariff barriers.

- – – Boundary of Austria-Hungary 1867-1918
- ▬▬ New Boundaries of 1919.
- ══ Main railway lines.

C Z E C H O S L O V A K I A

R U S S I A

Miles
0   50   100

Vienna
FROM CZECHOSLOVAKIA 1938–1945
FROM CZECHOSLOVAKIA 1939–1945
Bratislava
Miskolc
Chust
A U S T R I A
Sopron
Gyor
Debrecen
FROM RUMANIA 1941–1945
Budapest
H U N G A R Y
1920-1938 and since 1945
Kolozsvar (Cluj)
Szeged
Arad
Pecs
Subotica
Temisoara
Zagreb (Agram)
FROM YUGOSLAVIA 1941–1945
Brasov
Fiume
Y U G O S L A V I A
Belgrade
R U M A N I A

HUNGARY since 1867

- ▬▬ Boundary of Hungary, 1867-1918.
- ‖‖‖ Territory lost in 1919
- ▬▬ Hungary as laid down by the Treaty of Trianon 1920.
- ⋮⋮⋮ Territory regained from 1938 and lost in 1945

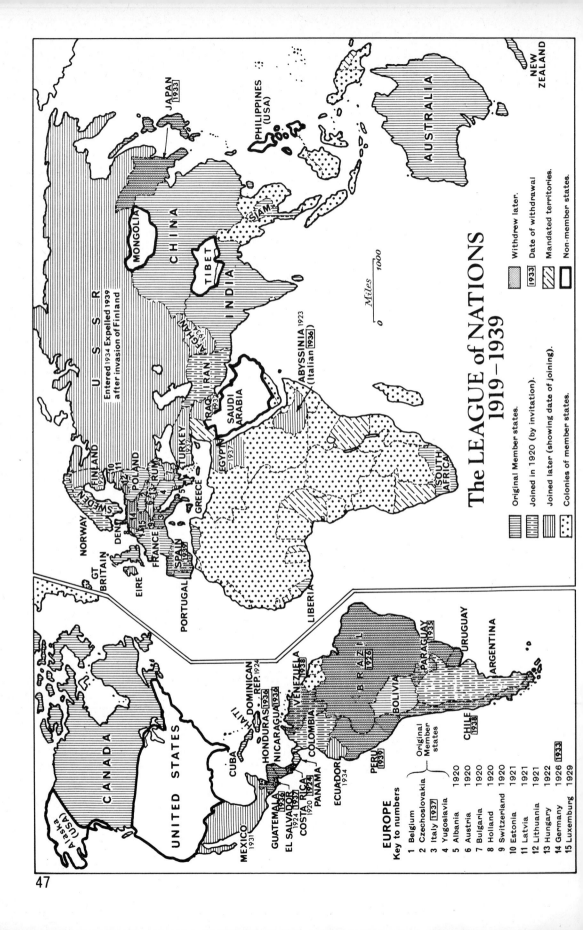

The LEAGUE of NATIONS 1919-1939

Legend:
- Original Member states.
- Joined in 1920 (by invitation).
- Joined later (showing date of joining).
- Colonies of member states.
- Withdrew later.
- 1933 Date of withdrawal
- Mandated territories.
- Non-member states.

Miles
0   1000

EUROPE
Key to numbers

Original Member states
1 Belgium
2 Czechoslovakia
3 Italy 1937
4 Yugoslavia
5 Albania   1920
6 Austria   1920
7 Bulgaria   1920
8 Holland   1920
9 Switzerland 1920
10 Estonia   1921
11 Latvia   1921
12 Lithuania 1921
13 Hungary   1922
14 Germany   1926 1933
15 Luxemburg 1929

Map labels:

ALASKA (USA)
CANADA
UNITED STATES
MEXICO 1931
GUATEMALA 1936
EL SALVADOR 1924 1937
COSTA RICA 1920 1925
PANAMA 1920
HONDURAS 1936
NICARAGUA 1936
CUBA
HAITI
DOMINICAN REP. 1924
VENEZUELA 1938
COLOMBIA
ECUADOR 1934
PERU 1939
BRAZIL 1926
BOLIVIA
PARAGUAY 1935
CHILE 1938
URUGUAY
ARGENTINA

NORWAY
SWEDEN
GT BRITAIN
EIRE
DENMARK
FRANCE
PORTUGAL
SPAIN 1939
GREECE
TURKEY
FINLAND
POLAND
RUM.

U S S R
Entered 1934 Expelled 1939
after invasion of Finland

JAPAN 1933
MONGOLIA
CHINA
TIBET
INDIA
SIAM
AFGHANISTAN
IRAN
IRAQ 1932
SAUDI ARABIA
EGYPT 1937
ABYSSINIA 1923 (Italian 1936)
LIBERIA
SOUTH AFRICA

PHILIPPINES (USA)
AUSTRALIA
NEW ZEALAND

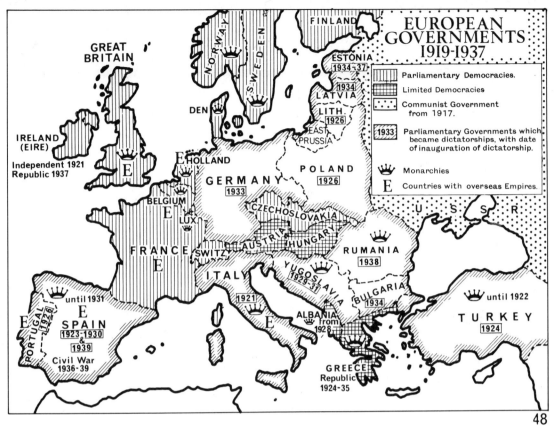

EUROPEAN GOVERNMENTS 1919-1937

⦀	Parliamentary Democracies.
▦	Limited Democracies
⋰	Communist Government from 1917.
1933	Parliamentary Governments which became dictatorships, with date of inauguration of dictatorship.
♔	Monarchies
E	Countries with overseas Empires.

GREAT BRITAIN

IRELAND (EIRE)
Independent 1921
Republic 1937

NORWAY

S-W-E-D-E-N

FINLAND

ESTONIA
1934-37

LATVIA
1934

DEN

LITH.
1926

EAST PRUSSIA

HOLLAND

GERMANY
1933

POLAND
1926

U. S. S. R.

BELGIUM

LUX

CZECHOSLOVAKIA

FRANCE

SWITZ.

AUSTRIA HUNGARY

RUMANIA
1938

ITALY

YUGOSLAVIA
1929-31

BULGARIA
1934

PORTUGAL
1926

SPAIN
1923-1930
&
1939
Civil War
1936-39

until 1931

ITALY
1921

ALBANIA
from
1928

until 1922

TURKEY
1924

GREECE
Republic
1924-35

48

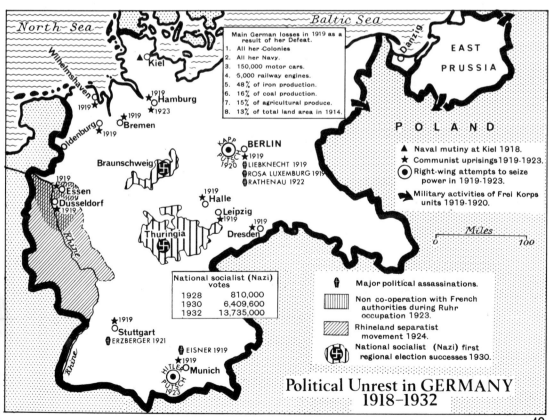

North Sea

Baltic Sea

Wilhelmshaven

Kiel

Hamburg
1919
1923

Oldenburg
1919

Bremen
1919

Braunschweig

KAPP PUTSCH 1920

BERLIN
1919
LIEBKNECHT 1919
ROSA LUXEMBURG 1919
RATHENAU 1922

Essen
1919

Dusseldorf
1919

Halle
1919

Leipzig
1919

Thuringia

Dresden
1919

Stuttgart
1919
ERZBERGER 1921

EISNER 1919

HITLER PUTSCH 1923

Munich
1919

Danzig

EAST PRUSSIA

POLAND

Rhine

Main German losses in 1919 as a result of her Defeat.
1. All her Colonies.
2. All her Navy.
3. 150,000 motor cars.
4. 5,000 railway engines.
5. 48% of iron production.
6. 16% of coal production.
7. 15% of agricultural produce.
8. 13% of total land area in 1914.

▲ Naval mutiny at Kiel 1918.
★ Communist uprisings 1919-1923.
◉ Right-wing attempts to seize power in 1919-1923.
➤ Military activities of Frei Korps units 1919-1920.

Miles
0 _____ 100

National socialist (Nazi) votes
1928	810,000
1930	6,409,600
1932	13,735,000

⬛ Major political assassinations.

⦀ Non co-operation with French authorities during Ruhr occupation 1923.

▨ Rhineland separatist movement 1924.

⊕ National socialist (Nazi) first regional election successes 1930.

Political Unrest in GERMANY 1918-1932

49

GERMAN EXPANSION 1935-July 1939

North Sea

Baltic Sea

Memel

LITHUANIA

○Vilna

Danzig

Königsberg

○Minsk

HOLLAND

Hamburg

G   E   R

BELGIUM

Cologne

RHINELAND

Frankfurt

LUX.

SAARLAND

M   A   N   Y

Berlin

Poznan
(Posen)

○Warsaw

○Brest
Litovsk

P   O   L   A   N   D

○Lublin

Leipzig

Breslau

○Cracow

FRANCE

C   Z   E   C

Eger

Bohemia

Moravia

H   O   -   S   L   O   V   A   K   I   A

Ruthenia

○Lvov
(Lemberg)

Munich

Berchtesgaden

Vienna

Bratislava
(Pressburg)

AUSTRIA

Budapest

HUNGARY

RUSSIA

RUMANIA

SWITZERLAND

ITALY

Miles
0 ——— 100

	GERMANY 1933
	Gained by Plebiscite 1935
	Remilitarized 1936
	Annexed 1938
	Annexed 1939
	Protectorate established 1939

50

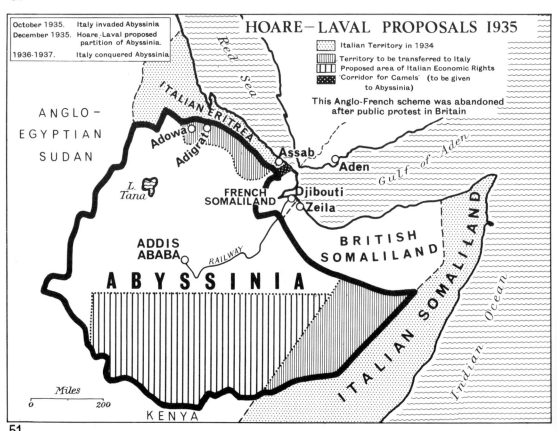

October 1935.   Italy invaded Abyssinia
December 1935. Hoare-Laval proposed
                partition of Abyssinia.
1936-1937.   Italy conquered Abyssinia

HOARE—LAVAL PROPOSALS 1935

	Italian Territory in 1934
	Territory to be transferred to Italy
	Proposed area of Italian Economic Rights
	'Corridor for Camels' (to be given to Abyssinia)

This Anglo-French scheme was abandoned
after public protest in Britain

Red Sea

ITALIAN ERITREA

ANGLO-
EGYPTIAN
SUDAN

Adowa○

Adigrat○

Assab

Gulf of Aden

Aden

FRENCH
SOMALILAND

Djibouti

Zeila

L.
Tana

BRITISH
SOMALILAND

ADDIS
ABABA

RAILWAY

A   B   Y   S   S   I   N   I   A

ITALIAN SOMALILAND

Indian Ocean

Miles
0 ——— 200

KENYA

51

JAPANESE EXPANSION
1931–1942

JAPAN 1928

Conquered by Japan 1929-1939

Conquered by Japan 1940-1942

1942 Dates of Japanese Conquest

Allied with Japan 1941.

Furthest extent of Japanese conquest 1942

Miles

0   1000

U S S R

MONGOLIA

U S S R

Japanese clashes with Russians 1939

MANCHURIA
1931-32

SAKHALIN

1200 miles
To KISKA I.
(USA)
1942

MANCHUKUO
1934

Mukden

Vladivostok

KURIL IS.

CHINA

Peking
1937

KOREA

Tokyo

Pacific Ocean

Kaifeng
1938

JAPAN

Hankow 1938

Shanghai
1937

Chungking

Yangtse

Nanchang 1942
1939

RYUKYU
IS.
OKINAWA

Bonin Is.
(Japan)

Kazan Is.
(Japan)

500 miles to
WAKE I.
(USA)
1941

TIBET

Amoy
1938
Swatow 1938
Canton 1938

FORMOSA

INDIA

Hong
Kong 1941
(British)

Mariana
Is.

BURMA
1942

Hanoi

HAINAN

Rangoon

SIAM

FRENCH
INDO-CHINA

Manila
1942

PHILIPPINE IS.
(USA)

Guam
(USA)
1941

JAPANESE MANDATE
from 1920

ANDAMAN
IS
(British)
1942

1940-41

Saigon

MINDANAO
1941

Caroline Is.

NICOBAR
IS
(British)
1942

N
BORNEO
1942
BRUNEI

1000 miles to
GILBERT IS.
(British)
1942

MALAYA
1942

SARAWAK
1941-42

Singapore
15·2·42

BORNEO
1942

AUSTRALIAN

MANDATE
from
1920

SUMATRA 1942

DUTCH

Djakarta
1942

EAST INDIES

NEW
GUINEA

New
Britain

Solomon Is.
(British)
1942

JAVA

TIMOR
1942

Port
Moresby

1942

*Timor
Sea* Darwin

*Coral
Sea*

Indian Ocean

AUSTRALIA

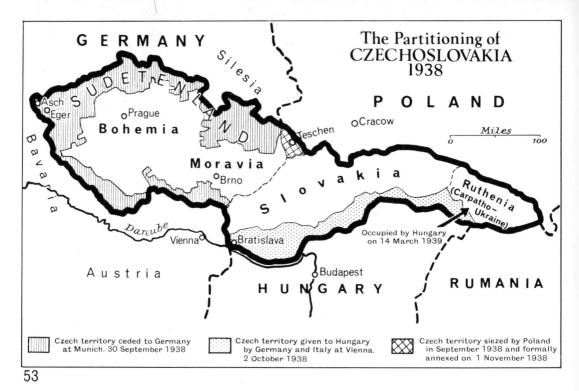

The Partitioning of CZECHOSLOVAKIA 1938

G E R M A N Y

Silesia

P O L A N D

S U D E T E N L A N D

Asch
Eger
Bohemia
Prague

Bavaria

oCracow

Teschen

Moravia

Brno

S l o v a k i a

Ruthenia
(Carpatho-Ukraine)

Danube

Vienna

Bratislava

Occupied by Hungary
on 14 March 1939

Miles
0   100

A u s t r i a

Budapest

H U N G A R Y

R U M A N I A

| | Czech territory ceded to Germany at Munich, 30 September 1938 | | Czech territory given to Hungary by Germany and Italy at Vienna, 2 October 1938 | | Czech territory siezed by Poland in September 1938 and formally annexed on 1 November 1938 |

53

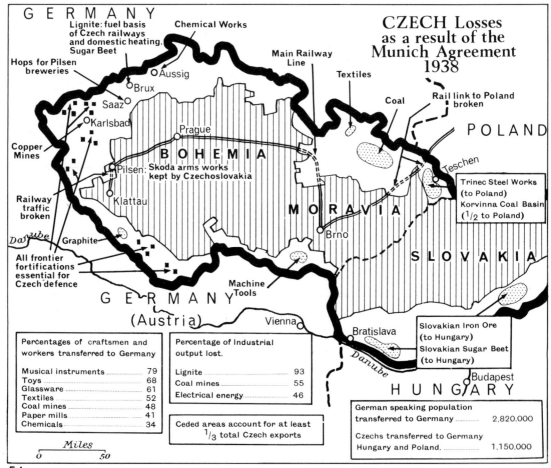

CZECH Losses as a result of the Munich Agreement 1938

G E R M A N Y

Lignite: fuel basis of Czech railways and domestic heating. Sugar Beet

Chemical Works

Main Railway Line

Hops for Pilsen breweries

oAussig

Textiles

Coal

Rail link to Poland broken

Brux

Saaz

Karlsbad

Prague

P O L A N D

Copper Mines

B O H E M I A

Teschen

Pilsen
Skoda arms works kept by Czechoslovakia

Trinec Steel Works (to Poland)
Korvinna Coal Basin (½ to Poland)

Railway traffic broken

Klattau

M O R A V I A

Danube

Graphite

Brno

S L O V A K I A

All frontier fortifications essential for Czech defence

Machine Tools

G E R M A N Y
(Austria)

Vienna

Bratislava

Slovakian Iron Ore (to Hungary)
Slovakian Sugar Beet (to Hungary)

Danube

Budapest

H U N G A R Y

Percentages of craftsmen and workers transferred to Germany	
Musical instruments	79
Toys	68
Glassware	61
Textiles	52
Coal mines	48
Paper mills	41
Chemicals	34

Percentage of Industrial output lost.	
Lignite	93
Coal mines	55
Electrical energy	46

Ceded areas account for at least ⅓ total Czech exports

Miles
0   50

German speaking population transferred to Germany	2,820,000
Czechs transferred to Germany Hungary and Poland.	1,150,000

54

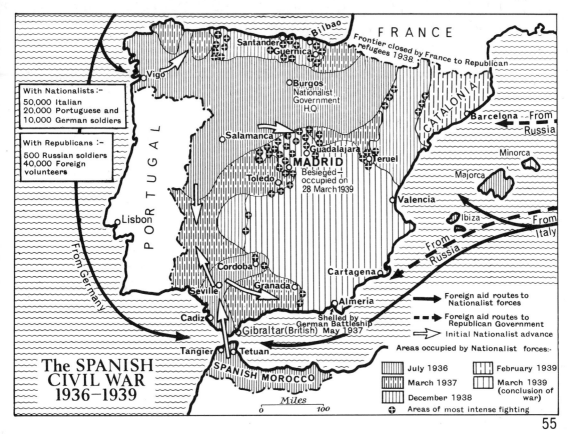

With Nationalists :-
50,000 Italian
20,000 Portuguese and
10,000 German soldiers

With Republicans :-
500 Russian soldiers
40,000 Foreign
volunteers

FRANCE

Frontier closed by France to Republican refugees 1938

Bilbao
Santander
Guernica
Vigo
Burgos
Nationalist Government HQ
CATALONIA
Barcelona From Russia
Salamanca
Guadalajara
MADRID Besieged occupied on 28 March 1939
Teruel
Minorca
Toledo
Valencia
Majorca
Ibiza
From Italy
Cordoba
From Russia
Cartagena
Granada
Almeria
Seville
Cadiz
Shelled by German Battleship
Gibraltar(British) May 1937
Tangier
Tetuan
SPANISH MOROCCO

PORTUGAL
Lisbon

From Germany

The SPANISH CIVIL WAR 1936-1939

Foreign aid routes to Nationalist forces
Foreign aid routes to Republican Government
Initial Nationalist advance

Areas occupied by Nationalist forces:-

July 1936	February 1939
March 1937	March 1939 (conclusion of war)
December 1938	

Miles
0   100

Areas of most intense fighting

SWITZERLAND
AUSTRIA 1938
BRENNER PASS
Budapest
HUNGARY

ITALIAN EXPANSION 1939 — 1943

Miles
0   100

FRANCE 1942
Milan
Turin
Venice
Trieste
SLOVENIA 1941
Belgrade
CROATIA
Occupied by Hungary
1941
Belgrade
RUMANIA

Nice (From France)
ITALY
YUGOSLAVIA
DALMATIA
BOSNIA
SERBIA 1941
BULGARIA
Sofia

CORSICA (From France)
Adriatic Sea
Cattaro (Kotor)
ALBANIA
MACEDONIA 1941
Occupied by Bulgaria
1941

ROME
Durazzo
Valona

SARDINIA
Naples

Tyrrhenian Sea

GREECE 1941

Aegean Sea

Ionian Sea

Palermo
SICILY

Athens

ITALY   January 1939.
Occupied by Italy April 1939.
Occupied by Italy 1940-1943.
Occupied by Germany
Joint German-Italian occupation 1941-1943

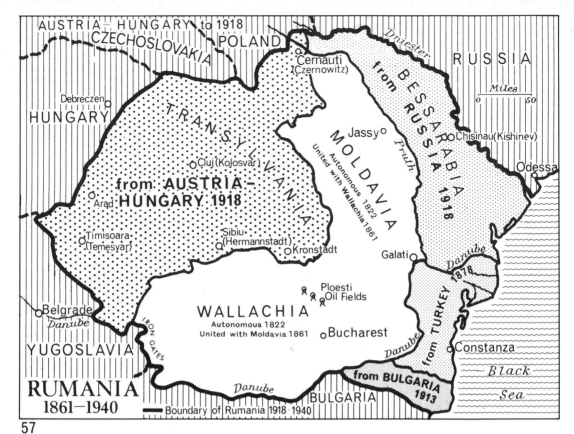

AUSTRIA—HUNGARY to 1918
CZECHOSLOVAKIA   POLAND

RUSSIA

Cernauti
(Czernowitz)

HUNGARY

Debreczen

Dniester

from BESSARABIA *RUSSIA*

Miles
0   50

TRANSYLVANIA

Chisinau(Kishinev)

Jassy

MOLDAVIA

Odessa

Cluj (Kolosvar)

Autonomous 1822
United with Wallachia 1861

Pruth

from AUSTRIA—
HUNGARY 1918

Arad

1918

Timisoara
(Temesvár)

Sibiu
(Hermannstadt)

Kronstadt

Galati

Danube 1878

from TURKEY

Ploesti
Oil Fields

WALLACHIA

Belgrade

Danube

Autonomous 1822
United with Moldavia 1861

Bucharest

Constanza

YUGOSLAVIA

IRON GATES

Danube

from BULGARIA
1913

*Black
Sea*

RUMANIA
1861—1940

Danube

—— Boundary of Rumania 1918-1940

BULGARIA

57

POLAND

Cernauti (Czernowitz)

Dniester

RUSSIA

RUSSIA since
1945

to and since 1945

HUNGARY

Debreczen

Miles
0   50

to HUNGARY
1940—1944 *TRANSYLVANIA*

Jassy

BESSARABIA 1940-1

Chisinau(Kishinev)

Oradea

Odessa

Cluj(Kolsovar)

Pruth

Arad

Timisoara
(Temesvar)

Sibiu(Hermannstadt)

Brasov
(Kronstadt)

Galati

Danube

Ploesti Oil
Fields

Belgrade

Danube

Craiova

Bucharest

Constanza

YUGOSLAVIA

IRON GATES

Danube

to BULGARIA
1940

*Black
Sea*

RUMANIA
since 1940

Danube

BULGARIA

—— Boundary of Rumania since 1944

58

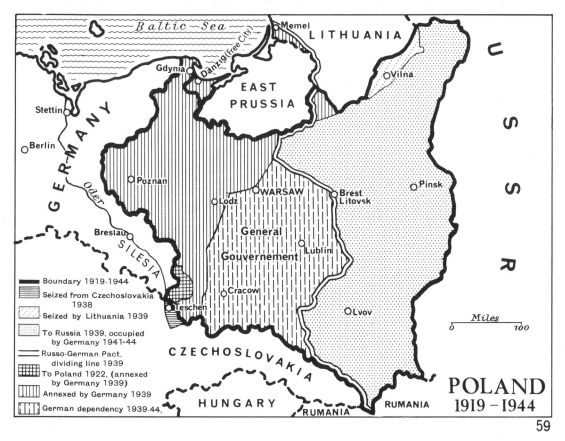

Legend (Poland 1919–1944):
- Boundary 1919–1944
- Seized from Czechoslovakia 1938
- Seized by Lithuania 1939
- To Russia 1939, occupied by Germany 1941–44
- Russo-German Pact, dividing line 1939
- To Poland 1922, (annexed by Germany 1939)
- Annexed by Germany 1939
- German dependency 1939–44.

POLAND
1919–1944

Baltic Sea · Memel · LITHUANIA · Gdynia · Danzig (Free City) · EAST PRUSSIA · Vilna · Stettin · GERMANY · Berlin · Oder · Poznan · WARSAW · Brest Litovsk · Pinsk · Lodz · Breslau · SILESIA · General Gouvernement · Lublin · Lvov · Cracow · Teschen · U.S.S.R · CZECHOSLOVAKIA · HUNGARY · RUMANIA · Miles 0 100

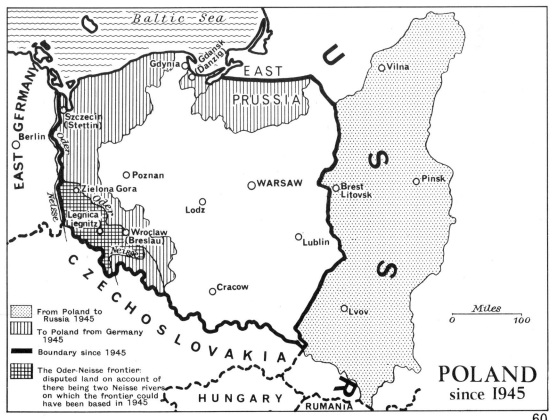

Legend (Poland since 1945):
- From Poland to Russia 1945
- To Poland from Germany 1945
- Boundary since 1945
- The Oder-Neisse frontier: disputed land on account of there being two Neisse rivers on which the frontier could have been based in 1945

POLAND
since 1945

Baltic Sea · Gdynia · Gdansk (Danzig) · EAST PRUSSIA · Vilna · EAST GERMANY · Szczecin (Stettin) · Berlin · Oder · Neisse · Poznan · WARSAW · Brest Litovsk · Pinsk · Zielona Gora · Lodz · Legnica Liegnitz · Wroclaw (Breslau) · Neisse · Lublin · Cracow · Lvov · U.S.S.R · CZECHOSLOVAKIA · HUNGARY · RUMANIA · Miles 0 100

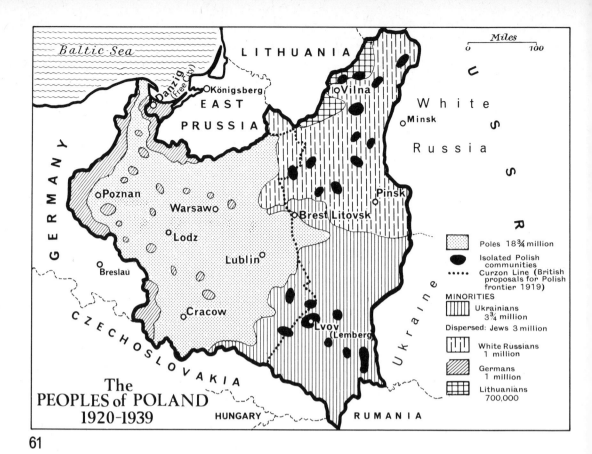

The PEOPLES of POLAND 1920-1939

Baltic Sea

LITHUANIA

Danzig (free City)

Königsberg

EAST PRUSSIA

GERMANY

Poznan

Warsaw

Lodz

Lublin

Breslau

CZECHOSLOVAKIA

Cracow

Lvov (Lemberg)

HUNGARY

Vilna

Minsk

White Russia

Pinsk

Brest Litovsk

U S S R

Ukraine

RUMANIA

Miles 0 100

Poles 18¾ million

Isolated Polish communities

Curzon Line (British proposals for Polish frontier 1919)

MINORITIES

Ukrainians 3¾ million

Dispersed: Jews 3 million

White Russians 1 million

Germans 1 million

Lithuanians 700,000

61

The FREE CITY of DANZIG 1919—1939

The Treaty of Versailles put Danzig " under the protection of the League of Nations " and " within the Polish customs Frontier ". Germany renounced all rights and claims in the Free City

Baltic Sea

TO MEMEL

Königsberg

TO VILNA

Miles 0 30

Hel Peninsula

Gulf of Danzig

GERMANY

Stolp

Gdynia

Zoppot

Danzig

Elbing

POLAND'S ONLY ACCESS TO THE SEA

Tczew

Marienburg

EAST PRUSSIA

POLAND (GERMANY before 1918)

Wisła

Allenstein

Main railways

Chojnice

Schmentau

Marienwerder

Free Territory of Danzig (annexed by Germany 1939)

'Corridor' sought by Germany

To Germany after Plebiscite 1922.

Deutsch Eylau

Grudziadz

TO BERLIN

TO POZNAN

TO WARSAW

62

The Relative Strength of the Powers January 1939

NORWAY
- 4
- 8
- 9
- 13,000
- 100

DENMARK
- 2
- 8
- 12,000
- 65

SWEDEN
- 8
- 16
- 16
- 30,000
- 260

GREAT BRITAIN
- 19
- 189
- 71
- 154,000 (volunteers)
- 2,800

HOLLAND
- 3
- 8
- 30
- 60,000
- 330

USA
- 15
- 196
- 84
- 166,000 (volunteers)
- 2,500

GERMANY
- 5
- 23
- 36
- 1,500,000
- 4,500

POLAND
- 4
- 6
- 600,000
- 800

RUSSIA
- 4
- 32
- 38
- 1,300,000
- 1,500

BELGIUM
- 80,000
- 210

FRANCE
- 5
- 38
- 76
- 700,000
- 2,500

CZECHOSLOVAKIA
- 180,000
- 560

SWITZ
- 50,000
- 200

HUNGARY
- 350,000 (volunteers)

RUMANIA
- 7
- 2
- 180,000
- 840

ITALY
- 4
- 110
- 82
- 850,000
- 2,000

YUGOSLAVIA
- 2
- 4
- 190,000
- 800

BULGARIA
- 20,000

Legend:
- Battleships
- Destroyers
- Submarines
- Soldiers
- Aircraft

Miles 0 — 100

Silesia · Sudetenland · Austria

63

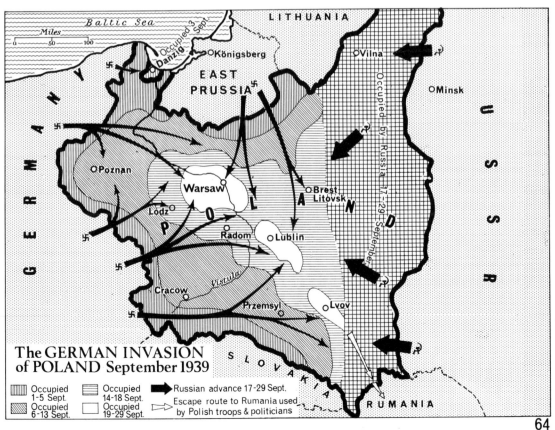

The GERMAN INVASION of POLAND September 1939

LITHUANIA · Baltic Sea · Miles 0 50 100

Occupied 3 Sept. · Danzig · Königsberg · Vilna · Minsk

EAST PRUSSIA

GERMANY · Poznan · Warsaw · Lodz · Brest Litovsk · Radom · Lublin · Cracow · Vistula · Przemysl · Lvov

Occupied by Russia 17–29 September

U S S R

SLOVAKIA · RUMANIA

Legend:
- Occupied 1–5 Sept.
- Occupied 6–13 Sept.
- Occupied 14–18 Sept.
- Occupied 19–29 Sept.
- Russian advance 17–29 Sept.
- Escape route to Rumania used by Polish troops & politicians

64

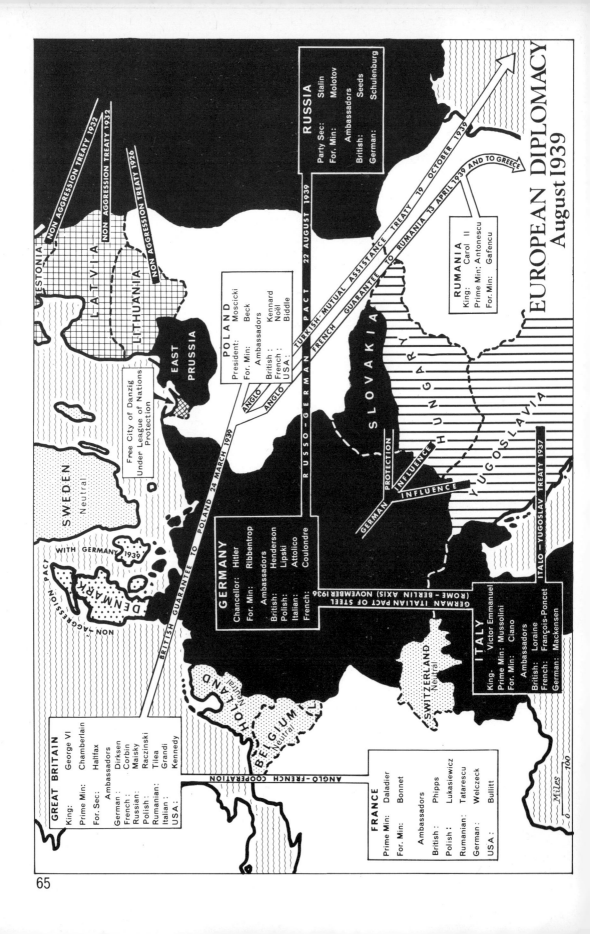

EUROPEAN DIPLOMACY
August 1939

RUSSIA
Party Sec: Stalin
For. Min: Molotov
Ambassadors
British: Seeds
German: Schulenburg

RUMANIA
King: Carol II
Prime Min: Antonescu
For. Min: Gafencu

POLAND
President: Mościcki
For. Min: Beck
Ambassadors
British : Kennard
French : Noël
USA : Biddle

GERMANY
Chancellor: Hitler
For. Min: Ribbentrop
Ambassadors
British: Henderson
Polish: Lipski
Italian: Attolico
French: Coulondre

ITALY
King: Victor Emmanuel
Prime Min: Mussolini
For. Min: Ciano
Ambassadors
British: Loraine
French: François-Poncet
German: Mackensen

GREAT BRITAIN
King: George VI
Prime Min: Chamberlain
For. Sec: Halifax
Ambassadors
German : Dirksen
French : Corbin
Russian: Maisky
Polish: Raczinski
Rumanian: Tilea
Italian : Grandi
USA: Kennedy

FRANCE
Prime Min: Daladier
For. Min: Bonnet
Ambassadors
British : Phipps
Polish : Lukasiewicz
Rumanian: Tatarescu
German : Welczeck
USA : Bullitt

Free City of Danzig
Under League of Nations
Protection

RUSSO-GERMAN PACT 22 AUGUST 1939

TURKISH-FRENCH GUARANTEE TO RUMANIA 13 APRIL 1939 AND TO GREECE

MUTUAL ASSISTANCE TREATY 19 OCTOBER 1939

BRITISH GUARANTEE TO POLAND 24 MARCH 1939

NON AGGRESSION TREATY 1932

NON AGGRESSION TREATY 1932

NON AGGRESSION TREATY 1926

NON AGGRESS'ON PACT

WITH GERMANY 1939

GERMAN ITALIAN PACT OF STEEL
(ROME-BERLIN AXIS) NOVEMBER 1936

ITALO-YUGOSLAV TREATY 1937

ANGLO

ANGLO

GERMAN PROTECTION

GERMAN INFLUENCE

INFLUENCE

ANGLO-FRENCH COOPERATION

ESTONIA

LATVIA

LITHUANIA

EAST PRUSSIA

SWEDEN
Neutral

DENMARK

HOLLAND
Neutral

BELGIUM
Neutral

SWITZERLAND
Neutral

SLOVAKIA

HUNGARY

YUGOSLAVIA

Miles
0   100

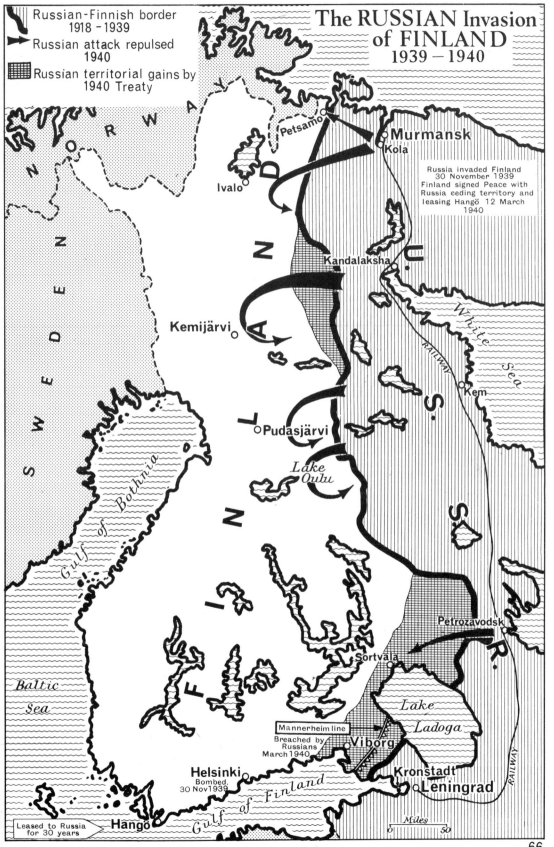

The RUSSIAN Invasion of FINLAND 1939 – 1940

Russian-Finnish border 1918 - 1939

Russian attack repulsed 1940

Russian territorial gains by 1940 Treaty

Russia invaded Finland 30 November 1939 Finland signed Peace with Russia ceding territory and leasing Hangö 12 March 1940

NORWAY

SWEDEN

FINLAND

U.S.S.R.

Petsamo

Murmansk

Kola

Ivalo

Kandalaksha

White Sea

Kemijärvi

RAILWAY

Kem

Pudasjärvi

Lake Oulu

Gulf of Bothnia

Petrozavodsk

Sortvala

Baltic Sea

Lake Ladoga

Mannerheim line
Breached by Russians March 1940

Viborg

RAILWAY

Kronstadt

Helsinki
Bombed, 30 Nov 1939

Leningrad

Gulf of Finland

Leased to Russia for 30 years

Hangö

Miles
0   50

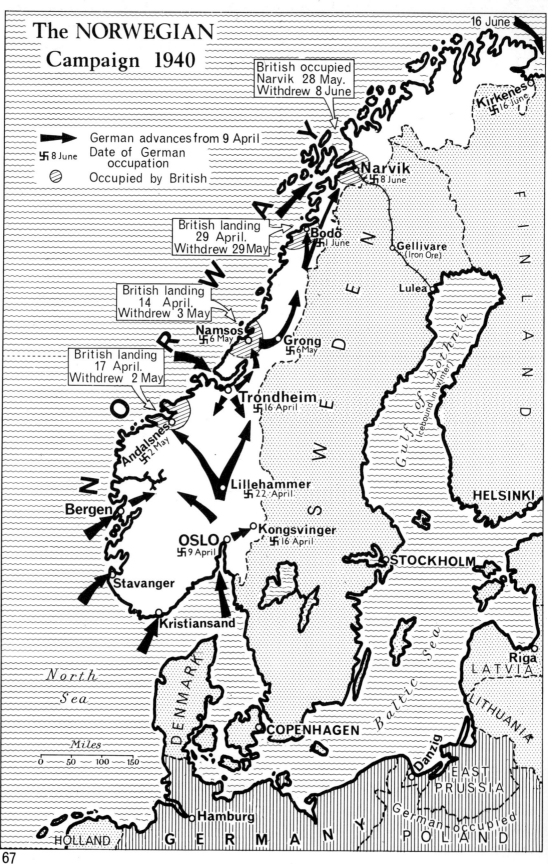

The NORWEGIAN
Campaign 1940

British occupied
Narvik 28 May.
Withdrew 8 June

➤ German advances from 9 April
卐 8 June Date of German occupation
⊘ Occupied by British

British landing
29 April.
Withdrew 29 May

British landing
14 April.
Withdrew 3 May

British landing
17 April.
Withdrew 2 May

Kirkenes 卐 16 June

16 June

N O R W A Y

Narvik 卐 8 June

Bodo 卐 1 June

Gellivare
(Iron Ore)

Lulea

Namsos 卐 6 May

Grong 卐 6 May

Trondheim 卐 16 April

S W E D E N

Gulf of Bothnia
(Icebound in winter)

F I N L A N D

Andalsnes 卐 2 May

Lillehammer 卐 22 April

HELSINKI

Bergen

OSLO 卐 9 April

Kongsvinger 卐 16 April

STOCKHOLM

Stavanger

Kristiansand

North
Sea

DENMARK

Riga
LATVIA

LITHUANIA

Baltic Sea

Miles
0 50 100 150

COPENHAGEN

Danzig

EAST
PRUSSIA

German-occupied

Hamburg

HOLLAND

G E R M A N Y

POLAND

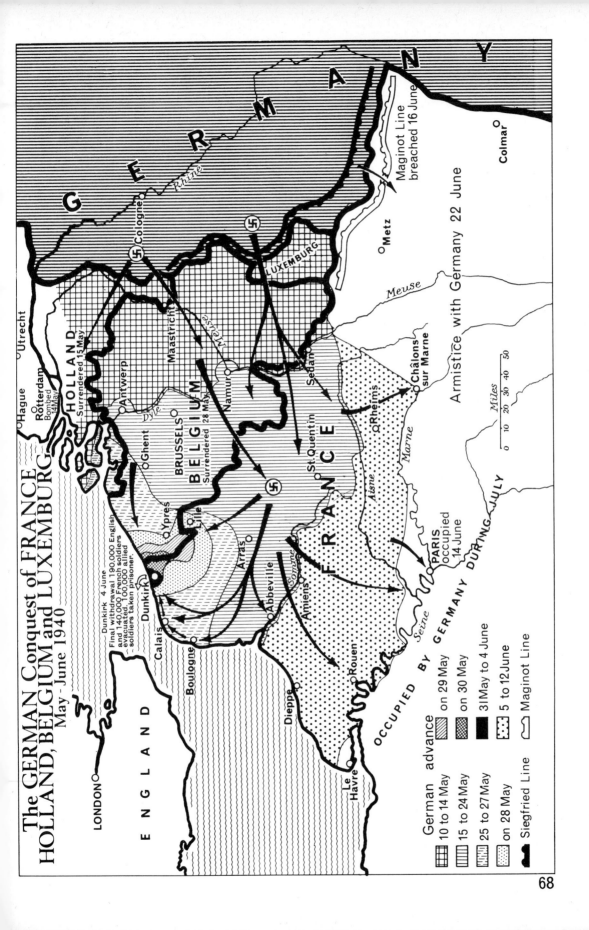

The GERMAN Conquest of FRANCE
HOLLAND, BELGIUM and LUXEMBURG,
May - June 1940

GERMANY

Maginot Line
breached 16 June

Armistice with Germany 22 June

Colmar

Metz

Meuse

Rhine

Cologne

LUXEMBURG

Châlons
sur Marne

Rheims

Marne

Aisne

Namur

Maastricht

Meuse

Sedan

St. Quentin

FRANCE

Dyle

BRUSSELS

BELGIUM
Surrendered 28 May

Ghent

HOLLAND
Surrendered 15 May

Antwerp

Rotterdam
Bombed
14 May

Hague

Utrecht

PARIS
occupied
14 June

Seine

Ypres

Lille

Arras

Abbeville

Somme

Amiens

Rouen

Dieppe

Boulogne

Calais

Dunkirk

Dunkirk 4 June
Final withdrawal 190,000 English
and 140,000 French soldiers
evacuated. 100,000 allied
soldiers taken prisoner.

LONDON

ENGLAND

Le
Havre

Miles
0 10 20 30 40 50

OCCUPIED BY GERMANY DURING JULY

German advance
10 to 14 May
15 to 24 May
25 to 27 May
on 28 May
Siegfried Line

on 29 May
on 30 May
31 May to 4 June
5 to 12 June
Maginot Line

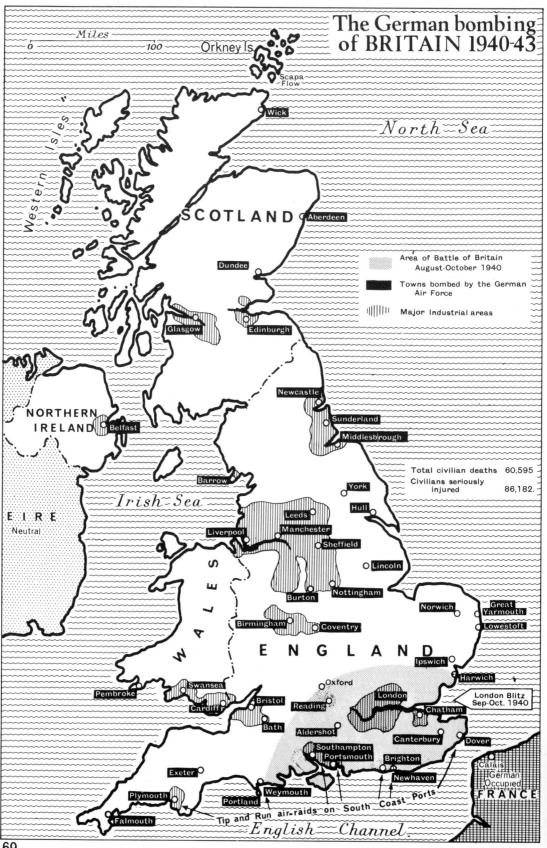

The German bombing of BRITAIN 1940-43

Miles
0   100

Orkney Is.

Scapa Flow

Wick

North Sea

SCOTLAND

Aberdeen

Area of Battle of Britain
August-October 1940

Towns bombed by the German
Air Force

Major Industrial areas

Dundee

Glasgow

Edinburgh

Newcastle

Sunderland

Middlesbrough

NORTHERN
IRELAND

Belfast

Total civilian deaths   60,595
Civilians seriously
        injured   86,182.

Barrow

Irish Sea

York

Hull

EIRE
Neutral

Leeds

Liverpool

Manchester

Sheffield

Lincoln

Nottingham

Burton

WALES

Birmingham

Coventry

Norwich

Great
Yarmouth

Lowestoft

ENGLAND

Ipswich

Swansea

Pembroke

Cardiff

Bristol

Reading

Oxford

London

Harwich

London Blitz
Sep-Oct. 1940

Bath

Aldershot

Chatham

Canterbury

Southampton

Portsmouth

Brighton

Dover

Exeter

Newhaven

Calais
German
Occupied
FRANCE

Plymouth

Portland

Weymouth

Falmouth

Tip and Run air-raids on South Coast Ports

English Channel

The GERMAN CONQUEST of
YUGOSLAVIA and GREECE
6-30 April 1941

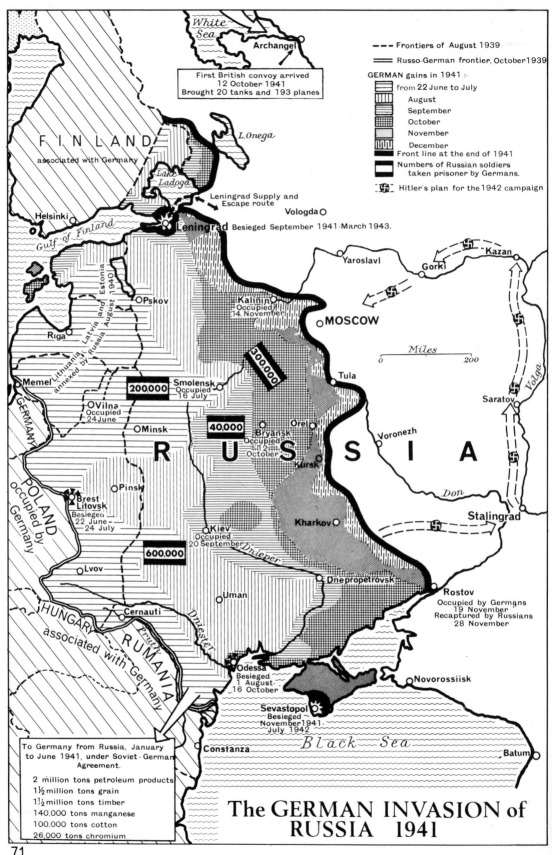

White
Sea

Archangel →

First British convoy arrived
12 October 1941
Brought 20 tanks and 193 planes

- - - Frontiers of August 1939
═══ Russo-German frontier, October 1939
GERMAN gains in 1941 :-
   from 22 June to July
   August
   September
   October
   November
   December
▬▬ Front line at the end of 1941
▬ Numbers of Russian soldiers
   taken prisoner by Germans.
⊞ Hitler's plan for the 1942 campaign

FINLAND
associated with Germany

L.Onega

Lake
Ladoga

Kazan

Helsinki

Gulf of Finland

Leningrad Supply and
Escape route

Vologda

Leningrad Besieged September 1941-March 1943.

Yaroslavl

Gorki

Pskov

Kalinin
Occupied
14 November

MOSCOW

Riga

Miles
0   200

Memel

Lithuania, Latvia and Estonia
annexed by Russia August 1940

300000

Tula

Saratov

Smolensk
Occupied
16 July

200,000

Vilna
Occupied
24 June

Minsk

40,000

Bryansk
Occupied
12
October

Orel

Voronezh

R U S S I A

Kursk

Don

GERMANY

POLAND
occupied by
Germany

Pinsk

Brest
Litovsk
Besieged
22 June -
24 July

Kiev
Occupied
20 September

600,000

Kharkov

Stalingrad

Lvov

Dnieper

Uman

Dnepropetrovsk

Rostov
Occupied by Germans
19 November
Recaptured by Russians
28 November

HUNGARY
associated with Germany

RUMANIA

Cernauti

Dniester

Prut

Novorossiisk

Odessa
Besieged
1 August -
16 October

Sevastopol
Besieged
November 1941-
July 1942

Constanza

Black Sea

Batum

To Germany from Russia, January
to June 1941, under Soviet-German
Agreement.

2 million tons petroleum products
1½ million tons grain
1½ million tons timber
140,000 tons manganese
100,000 tons cotton
26,000 tons chromium

The GERMAN INVASION of
RUSSIA   1941

71

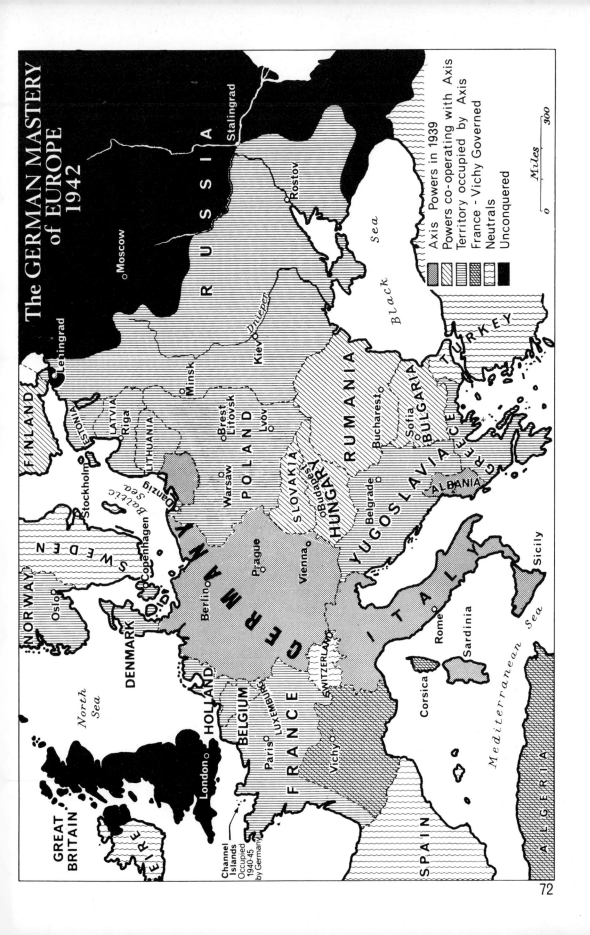

The GERMAN MASTERY of EUROPE 1942

Legend:
- Axis Powers in 1939
- Powers co-operating with Axis
- Territory occupied by Axis
- France - Vichy Governed
- Neutrals
- Unconquered

Miles
0   300

GREAT BRITAIN

EIRE

NORWAY

SWEDEN

FINLAND

DENMARK

HOLLAND

BELGIUM

LUXEMBURG

FRANCE

SWITZERLAND

GERMANY

SLOVAKIA

HUNGARY

POLAND

RUMANIA

YUGOSLAVIA

BULGARIA

GREECE

ALBANIA

ITALY

SPAIN

ALGERIA

TURKEY

RUSSIA

ESTONIA

LATVIA

LITHUANIA

London

Paris

Vichy

Oslo

Copenhagen

Stockholm

Berlin

Prague

Vienna

Budapest

Belgrade

Sofia

Bucharest

Warsaw

Danzig

Riga

Brest Litovsk

Lvov

Minsk

Kiev

Rostov

Leningrad

Moscow

Stalingrad

Rome

Corsica

Sardinia

Sicily

North Sea

Baltic Sea

Black Sea

Mediterranean Sea

Dnieper

Channel Islands Occupied 1940-45 by Germany

72

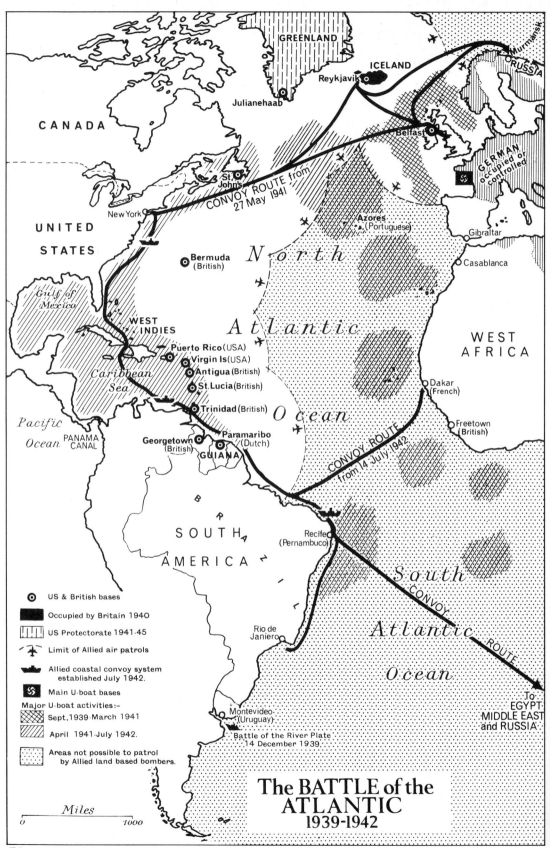

GREENLAND

ICELAND

Reykjavik

Julianehaab

Murmansk

RUSSIA

CANADA

Belfast

GERMAN occupied or controlled

St. John's

CONVOY ROUTE from 27 May 1941

New York

UNITED STATES

North

Azores
(Portuguese)

Gibraltar

Casablanca

Bermuda
(British)

Gulf of
Mexico

Atlantic

WEST
INDIES

WEST
AFRICA

Puerto Rico (USA)

Virgin Is (USA)

*Caribbean
Sea*

Antigua (British)

St. Lucia (British)

Ocean

Dakar
(French)

Trinidad (British)

Freetown
(British)

*Pacific
Ocean* PANAMA
CANAL

Paramaribo
(Dutch)

Georgetown
(British)

GUIANA

CONVOY ROUTE
from 14 July 1942

B
R
A
Z
I
L

SOUTH

AMERICA

Recife
(Pernambuco)

South

Atlantic

Rio de
Janiero

SOUTH CONVOY ROUTE

Ocean

US & British bases

Occupied by Britain 1940

US Protectorate 1941-45

Limit of Allied air patrols

Allied coastal convoy system
established July 1942.

Main U-boat bases

Major U-boat activities:–

Sept. 1939-March 1941

April 1941-July 1942.

Areas not possible to patrol
by Allied land based bombers.

Montevideo
(Uruguay)

To
EGYPT
MIDDLE EAST
and RUSSIA

Battle of the River Plate
14 December 1939

Miles

0   1000

The BATTLE of the ATLANTIC 1939-1942

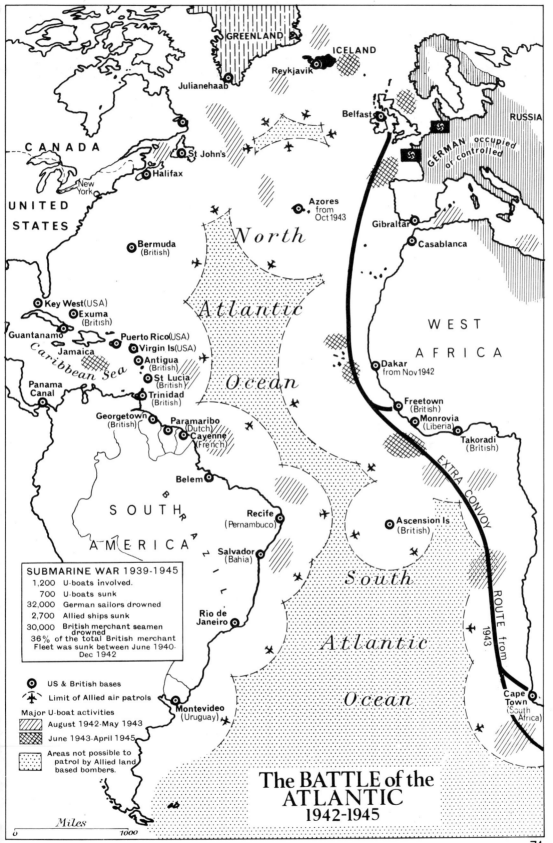

GREENLAND

ICELAND

Reykjavik

Julianehaab

CANADA

St John's

Halifax

New York

UNITED
STATES

Belfast

RUSSIA

GERMAN occupied
or controlled

Azores
from
Oct 1943

Gibraltar

Casablanca

North

Bermuda
(British)

Atlantic

WEST

AFRICA

Key West (USA)

Exuma
(British)

Guantanamo

Puerto Rico (USA)

Jamaica

Virgin Is (USA)

Antigua
(British)

St Lucia
(British)

Panama
Canal

Trinidad
(British)

Caribbean Sea

Georgetown
(British)

Paramaribo
(Dutch)

Cayenne
(French)

Ocean

Dakar
from Nov 1942

Freetown
(British)

Monrovia
(Liberia)

Takoradi
(British)

Belem

B
R
A
Z
I
L

SOUTH

AMERICA

Recife
(Pernambuco)

Ascension Is.
(British)

Salvador
(Bahia)

EXTRA CONVOY

South

SUBMARINE WAR 1939-1945
1,200 U-boats involved.
  700 U-boats sunk
32,000 German sailors drowned
 2,700 Allied ships sunk
30,000 British merchant seamen
         drowned
36% of the total British merchant
   Fleet was sunk between June 1940-
           Dec 1942

Rio de
Janeiro

Atlantic

ROUTE from 1943

⊙ US & British bases

✈ Limit of Allied air patrols

Major U-boat activities

▨ August 1942-May 1943

▨ June 1943-April 1945

⬚ Areas not possible to
    patrol by Allied land
    based bombers.

Ocean

Montevideo
(Uruguay)

Cape
Town
(South
Africa)

The BATTLE of the
ATLANTIC
1942-1945

Miles

0   1000

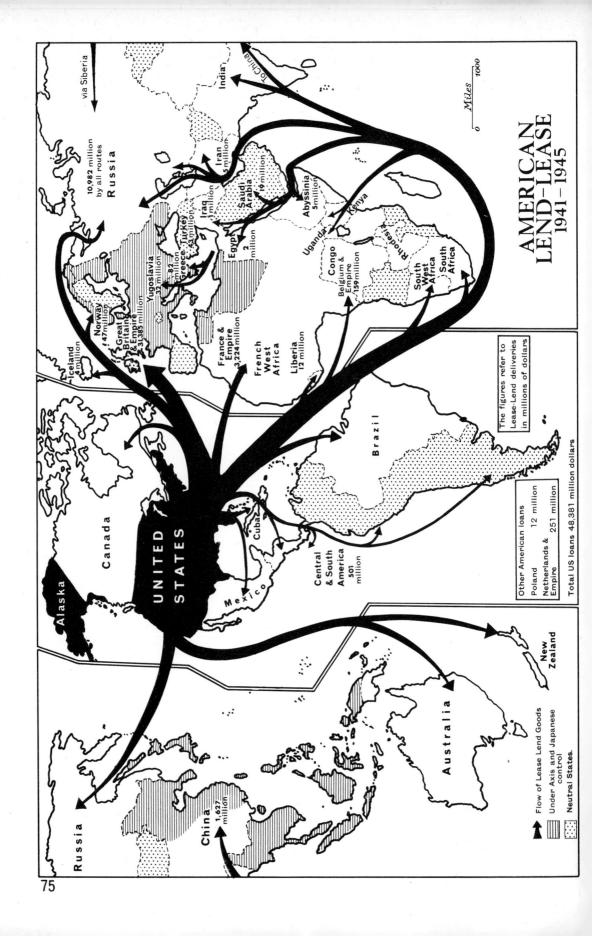

AMERICAN
LEND-LEASE
1941-1945

Miles
0   1000

via Siberia

Russia
10,982 million
by all routes

India

To China

Iran
5 million

Iraq
1 million

Saudi
Arabia
19 million

Abyssinia
5 million

Kenya

Uganda

Congo
Belgium &
Empire
159 million

Rhodesia

South
West
Africa

South
Africa

Turkey
43 million

Greece
82 million

Yugoslavia
32 million

Egypt
2 million

Great Britain
& Empire
31,385 million

Norway
47 million

Iceland
4 million

France &
Empire
3,224 million

French
West
Africa

Liberia
12 million

Brazil

The figures refer to
Lease-Lend deliveries
in millions of dollars

Alaska

Canada

UNITED
STATES

Cuba

Mexico

Central
& South
America
501
million

New
Zealand

Australia

Russia

China
1,627
million

Other American loans
Poland   12 million
Netherlands &
Empire   251 million

Total US loans 48,381 million dollars

Flow of Lease Lend Goods

Under Axis and Japanese
control

Neutral States.

75

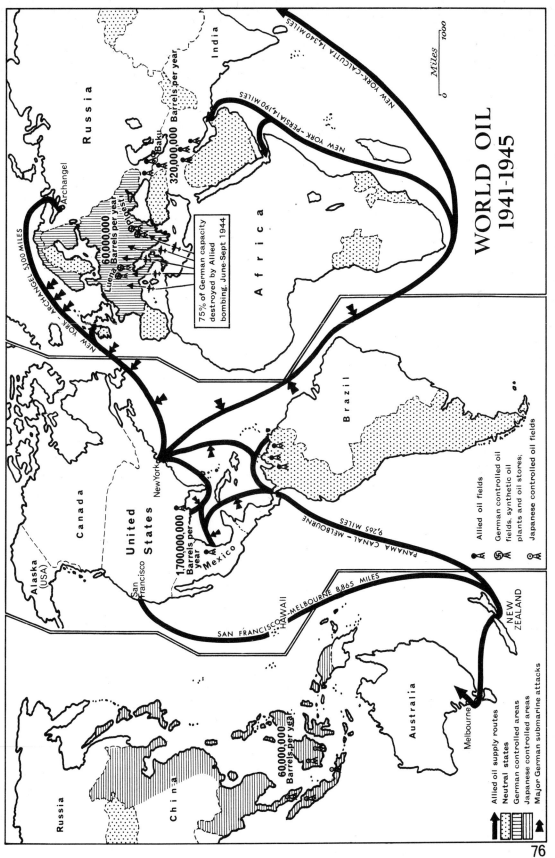

WORLD OIL
1941-1945

75% of German capacity
destroyed by Allied
bombing, June–Sept 1944

320,000,000 Barrels per year

60,000,000 Barrels per year

1,700,000,000 Barrels per year

60,000,000 Barrels per year

NEW YORK–CALCUTTA 14,340 MILES

NEW YORK–PERSIA 14,190 MILES

ARCHANGEL 5,100 MILES

NEW YORK–ARCHANGEL 5,100 MILES

PANAMA CANAL–MELBOURNE 9,265 MILES

SAN FRANCISCO–HAWAII–MELBOURNE 8,865 MILES

Russia

India

Africa

Brazil

Canada

United States

Alaska (USA)

Mexico

Baku

Archangel

New York

San Francisco

Australia

NEW ZEALAND

Melbourne

Russia

China

Miles
0   1000

Allied oil fields
German controlled oil fields, synthetic oil plants and oil stores;
Japanese controlled oil fields

Allied oil supply routes
Neutral states
German controlled areas
Japanese controlled areas
Major German submarine attacks

76

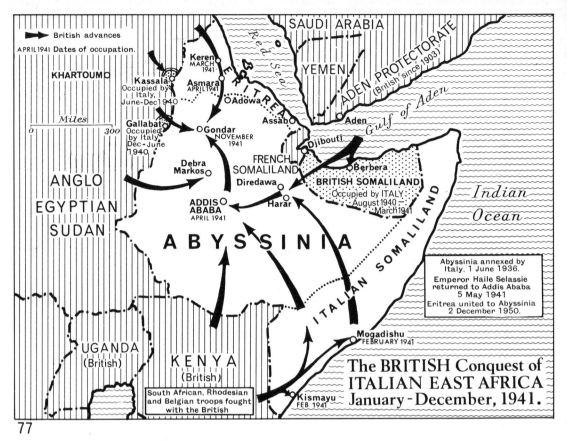

British advances
APRIL 1941 Dates of occupation.

SAUDI ARABIA

Red Sea

YEMEN

ADEN PROTECTORATE
(British since 1903)

KHARTOUM○

Keren
MARCH
1941

Kassala
Occupied by
Italy,
June-Dec 1940

Asmara
APRIL 1941

○Adowa

Assab○

Aden

Gulf of Aden

Gallabat
Occupied
by Italy
Dec-June
1940

○Gondar
NOVEMBER
1941

Djibouti

ERITREA

FRENCH
SOMALILAND

Berbera

BRITISH SOMALILAND
Occupied by ITALY
August 1940 –
March 1941

Debra
Markos○

Diredawa

*Indian
Ocean*

ANGLO
EGYPTIAN
SUDAN

ADDIS
ABABA
APRIL 1941

Harar

ITALIAN SOMALILAND

A B Y S S I N I A

Abyssinia annexed by
Italy, 1 June 1936.
Emperor Haile Selassie
returned to Addis Ababa
5 May 1941
Eritrea united to Abyssinia
2 December 1950.

Miles
0   300

UGANDA
(British)

KENYA
(British)

South African, Rhodesian
and Belgian troops fought
with the British

Mogadishu
FEBRUARY 1941

Kismayu
FEB 1941

The BRITISH Conquest of ITALIAN EAST AFRICA January – December, 1941.

77

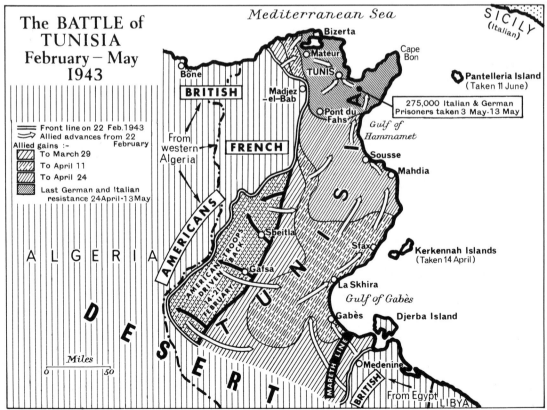

The BATTLE of TUNISIA February – May 1943

Mediterranean Sea

SICILY
(Italian)

Bizerta

○Mateur

Cape
Bon

Bône

TUNIS

Pantelleria Island
(Taken 11 June)

BRITISH

Madjez
-el-Bab

Front line on 22 Feb. 1943
Allied advances from 22
February
Allied gains :–
To March 29
To April 11
To April 24
Last German and Italian
resistance 24 April-13 May

From
western
Algeria

FRENCH

Pont du
Fahs

275,000 Italian & German
Prisoners taken 3 May-13 May

*Gulf of
Hammamet*

Sousse

Mahdia

A L G E R I A

AMERICANS

AMERICAN TROOPS DRIVEN BACK 14-21 FEBRUARY

Sbeitla

Gafsa

T U N I S I A

Sfax

Kerkennah Islands
(Taken 14 April)

La Skhira

Gulf of Gabès

Gabès

Djerba Island

D E S E R T

MARETH LINE

BRITISH

Medenine

From Egypt

LIBYA

Miles
0   50

78

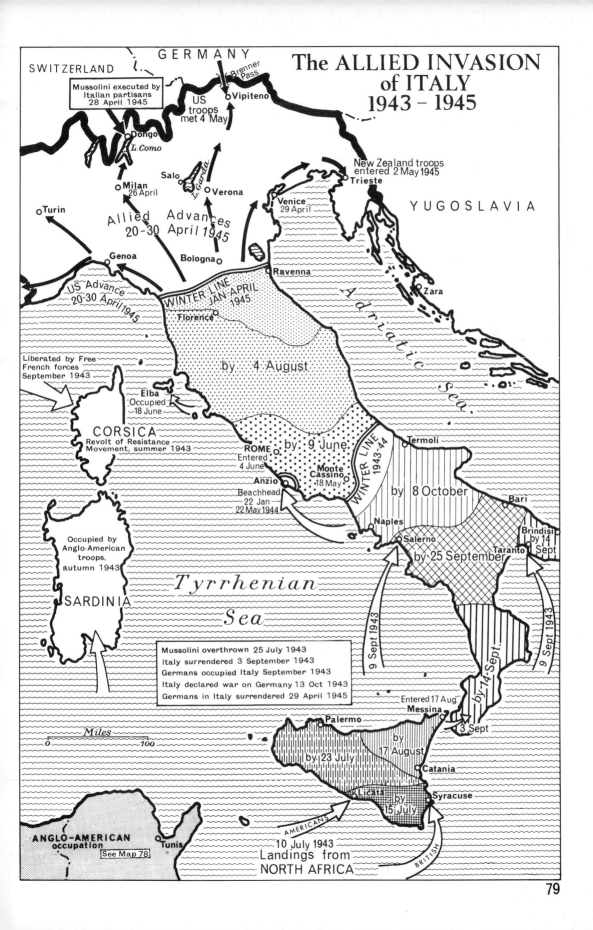

The ALLIED INVASION of ITALY 1943 – 1945

SWITZERLAND

GERMANY

Brenner Pass

Mussolini executed by
Italian partisans
28 April 1945

US troops
met 4 May

○Vipiteno

○Dongo
L.Como

US
troops
met 4 May

New Zealand troops
entered 2 May 1945

Salo

○Milan
26 April

L.Garda

○Verona

Venice
29 April

Trieste

YUGOSLAVIA

○Turin

Allied   Advances
20-30   April 1945

○Genoa

Bologna○

Ravenna

○Zara

US Advance
20-30 April 1945

WINTER LINE
JAN-APRIL
1945

Florence○

Adriatic Sea

Liberated by Free
French forces
September 1943

by 4 August

Elba
Occupied
18 June

CORSICA
Revolt of Resistance
Movement, summer 1943

ROME
Entered
4 June

by 9 June

Monte
Cassino
18 May

WINTER LINE 1943-44

Termoli○

by 8 October

Bari

Anzio○

Beachhead
22 Jan
22 May 1944

Naples

Salerno○

by 25 September

Brindisi
by 14
Sept

Taranto

Occupied by
Anglo-American
troops,
autumn 1943

Tyrrhenian

Sea

SARDINIA

9 Sept 1943

by 14 Sept.

9 Sept 1943

Mussolini overthrown 25 July 1943
Italy surrendered 3 September 1943
Germans occupied Italy September 1943
Italy declared war on Germany 13 Oct 1943
Germans in Italy surrendered 29 April 1945

Entered 17 Aug
Messina

Palermo○

by
17 August

3 Sept

by 23 July

Catania○

Miles
0   100

Licata
by
15 July

Syracuse○

ANGLO-AMERICAN
occupation
See Map 78

○Tunis

AMERICANS

10 July 1943
Landings from
NORTH AFRICA

BRITISH

79

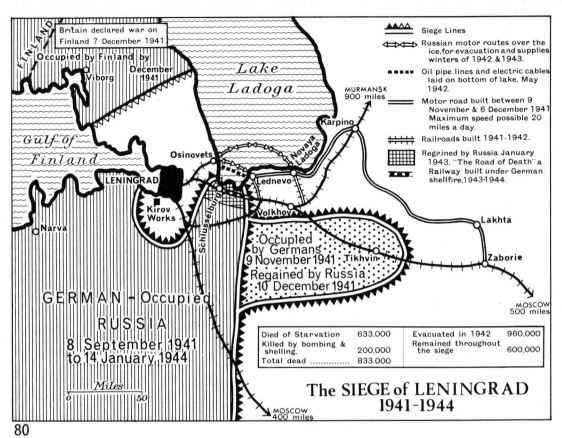

Britain declared war on
Finland 7 December 1941

Occupied by Finland by
December 1941

Siege Lines

**Russian motor routes over the
ice, for evacuation and supplies
winters of 1942 & 1943.**

**Oil pipe lines and electric cables
laid on bottom of lake, May
1942.**

**Motor road built between 9
November & 6 December 1941
Maximum speed possible 20
miles a day.**

Railroads built 1941-1942.

**Regained by Russia January
1943. "The Road of Death" a
Railway built under German
shellfire, 1943-1944.**

FINLAND

Viborg

*Lake
Ladoga*

*Gulf of
Finland*

MURMANSK
900 miles

Karpino

Osinovets

Novaya
Ladoga

Lednevo

LENINGRAD

Lakhta

Kirov
Works

Schlüsselburg

Volkhov

Zaborie

Narva

Occupied
by Germans
9 November 1941   Tikhvin
Regained by Russia
10 December 1941

MOSCOW
500 miles

GERMAN - Occupied
RUSSIA
8 September 1941
to 14 January, 1944

Died of Starvation	633,000	Evacuated in 1942	960,000
Killed by bombing & shelling.	200,000	Remained throughout the siege	600,000
Total dead	833,000		

Miles
0   50

The SIEGE of LENINGRAD
1941-1944

MOSCOW
400 miles

80

The RUSSIAN ADVANCE
1942-1944

FINLAND

Helsinki

*Lake
Ladoga*

SWEDEN
Neutral

G. of Finland

Leningrad

Baltic Sea

ESTONIA

Riga
LATVIA

Kalinin

Volga

Kazan

MOSCOW

Gorki

Memel
LITHUANIA

EAST
PRUSSIA

Vilna

Minsk

Berlin

GERMANY

Warsaw

Brest
Litovsk

Pinsk

Orel

Russo-German Frontier October 1939

Front line November 1942

Russian gains to April 1943

Retaken by Germans June-July 1943

Russian gains from July 1943-April 1944

German Controlled territory April 1944

Prague

POLAND

R U S S I A

Kiev

Kharkov

Don

Dnieper

Lvov

Stalingrad

Vienna

SLOVAKIA

Cernauti

Volga

Budapest

HUNGARY

Rostov

Astrakhan

Odessa

*Caspian
Sea*

YUGOSLAVIA

Belgrade

RUMANIA

Bucharest

Sevastopol

Black Sea

Grozny

BULGARIA

Miles
0   300

81

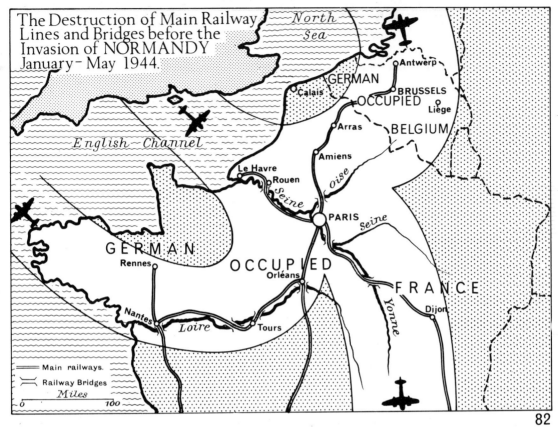

The Destruction of Main Railway
Lines and Bridges before the
Invasion of NORMANDY
January - May 1944.

North Sea

GERMAN
Antwerp
Calais
BRUSSELS
OCCUPIED
Liège
BELGIUM
Arras
Amiens
Oise

English Channel

Le Havre
Rouen
Seine
PARIS
Seine

GERMAN

Rennes

OCCUPIED
Orléans

FRANCE

Yonne
Dijon

Nantes
Loire
Tours

═══ Main railways.
⟋⟍ Railway Bridges
Miles
0   100

82

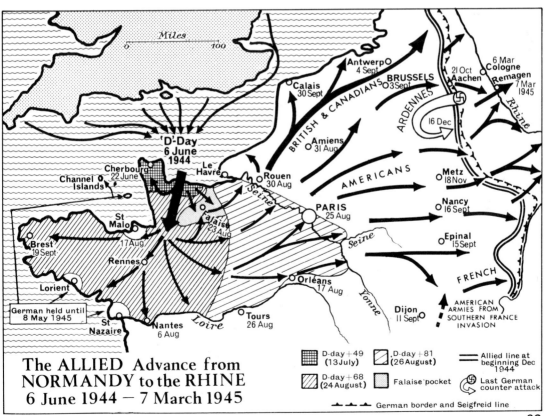

Miles
0   100

Antwerp
4 Sept
6 Mar
Cologne
21 Oct
Aachen
Remagen
Calais
30 Sept
BRUSSELS
3 Sept
7 Mar
1945
BRITISH & CANADIANS
ARDENNES
16 Dec
Rhine
'D'-Day
6 June
1944
Amiens
31 Aug
Cherbourg
22 June
Le Havre
Rouen
30 Aug
AMERICANS
Metz
18 Nov
Channel
Islands
Seine
St
Malo
Falaise
23 Aug
PARIS
25 Aug
Nancy
16 Sept
Brest
19 Sept
17 Aug
Seine
Epinal
15 Sept
Rennes
Lorient
Orléans
17 Aug
FRENCH
German held until
8 May 1945
St
Nazaire
Nantes
6 Aug
Loire
Tours
26 Aug
Yonne
Dijon
11 Sept
AMERICAN
ARMIES FROM
SOUTHERN FRANCE
INVASION

The ALLIED Advance from
NORMANDY to the RHINE
6 June 1944 – 7 March 1945

▦ D-day +49 (13 July) ▨ D-day +81 (26 August) ═══ Allied line at beginning Dec 1944
▧ D-day +68 (24 August) ▢ Falaise pocket ⟲ Last German counter attack
▲▲▲ German border and Seigfried line

83

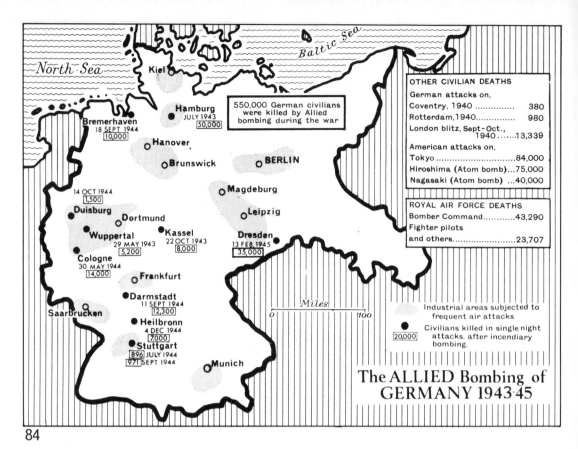

North Sea

Baltic Sea

Kiel

Hamburg
JULY 1943
50,000

Bremerhaven
18 SEPT 1944
10,000

Hanover

Brunswick

BERLIN

Magdeburg

Leipzig

14 OCT 1944
1,500
Duisburg
Dortmund

Wuppertal
29 MAY 1943
5,200

Kassel
22 OCT 1943
8,000

Dresden
13 FEB.1945
35,000

Cologne
30 MAY 1944
14,000

Frankfurt

Darmstadt
11 SEPT 1944
12,300

Saarbrucken

Heilbronn
4 DEC 1944
7,000

Stuttgart
896 JULY 1944
971 SEPT 1944

Munich

550,000 German civilians
were killed by Allied
bombing during the war

OTHER CIVILIAN DEATHS
German attacks on,
Coventry, 1940 380
Rotterdam,1940.............. 980
London blitz, Sept-Oct.,
1940 13,339
American attacks on,
Tokyo 84,000
Hiroshima (Atom bomb)...75,000
Nagasaki (Atom bomb) ...40,000

ROYAL AIR FORCE DEATHS
Bomber Command...........43,290
Fighter pilots
and others......................23,707

Miles
0   100

Industrial areas subjected to
frequent air attacks

20,000   Civilians killed in single night
attacks. after incendiary
bombing.

The ALLIED Bombing of
GERMANY 1943-45

84

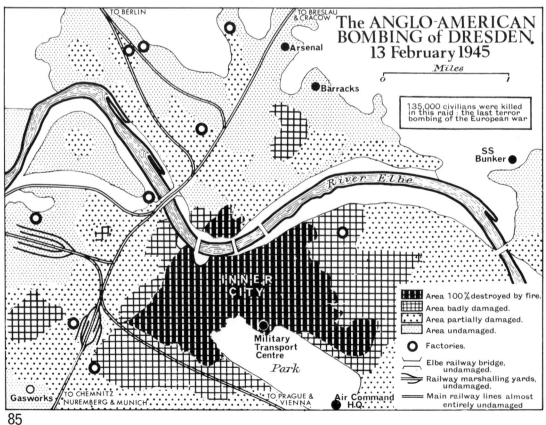

TO BERLIN

TO BRESLAU
& CRACOW

The ANGLO-AMERICAN
BOMBING of DRESDEN,
13 February 1945

Arsenal

Miles
0   1

Barracks

135,000 civilians were killed
in this raid : the last terror
bombing of the European war

SS
Bunker

River Elbe

INNER
CITY

Military
Transport
Centre

Park

Gasworks
TO CHEMNITZ
NUREMBERG & MUNICH

TO PRAGUE &
VIENNA

Air Command
H.Q.

Area 100% destroyed by fire.
Area badly damaged.
Area partially damaged.
Area undamaged.
Factories.
Elbe railway bridge,
undamaged.
Railway marshalling yards,
undamaged.
Main railway lines almost
entirely undamaged

85

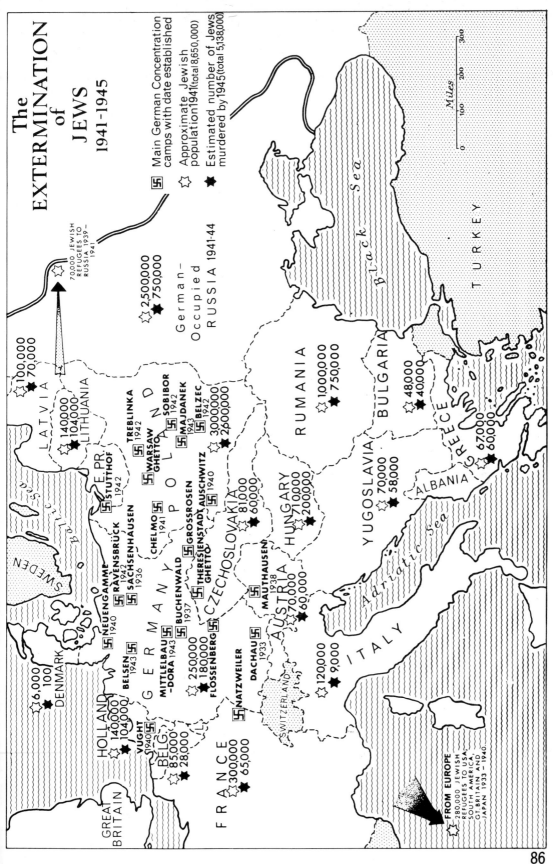

The
EXTERMINATION
of
JEWS
1941-1945

卐 Main German Concentration camps with date established

☆ Approximate Jewish population 1941 (total 8,650,000)

★ Estimated number of Jews murdered by 1945 (total 5,138,000)

Miles
0   100   200   300

70,000 JEWISH REFUGEES TO RUSSIA 1939—1941

☆ 2,500,000
★ 750,000

German-Occupied
RUSSIA 1941-44

☆ 100,000
★ 70,000
LATVIA

☆ 140,000
★ 104,000
LITHUANIA

E. PR.
卐 STUTTHOF 1942

卐 TREBLINKA 1942

卐 WARSAW GHETTO

卐 SOBIBOR 1942

P O L A N D

卐 MAJDANEK 1943

卐 BELZEC 1942

☆ 3,000,000
★ 2,600,000

卐 CHELMO 1941

卐 GROSSROSEN

卐 THERESIENSTADT GHETTO

卐 AUSCHWITZ 1940

CZECHOSLOVAKIA
☆ 81,000
★ 60,000

RUMANIA
☆ 1,000,000
★ 750,000

BULGARIA
☆ 48,000
★ 40,000

HUNGARY
☆ 710,000
★ 200,000

YUGOSLAVIA
☆ 70,000
★ 58,000

ALBANIA

GREECE
☆ 67,000
★ 60,000

T U R K E Y

Black Sea

卐 NEUENGAMME 1940

卐 RÄVENSBRÜCK 1942

卐 SACHSENHAUSEN 1936

BELSEN 1943

G E R M A N Y

卐 MITTELBAU–DORA 1943

卐 BUCHENWALD 1937

☆ 250,000
★ 180,000

卐 FLOSSENBERG

卐 MAUTHAUSEN

AUSTRIA 1938
☆ 70,000
★ 60,000

卐 DACHAU 1933

卐 NATZWEILER

☆ 120,000
★ 9,000

I T A L Y

Adriatic Sea

SWEDEN

Baltic Sea

DENMARK
☆ 6,000
★ 100

HOLLAND
☆ 140,000
★ 104,000

BELG.
☆ 85,000
★ 28,000

卐 VUGHT 1940

SWITZERLAND

F R A N C E
☆ 300,000
★ 65,000

GREAT BRITAIN

☆ FROM EUROPE
280,000 JEWISH REFUGEES TO USA, SOUTH AMERICA, GT. BRITAIN AND JAPAN 1933—1940

86

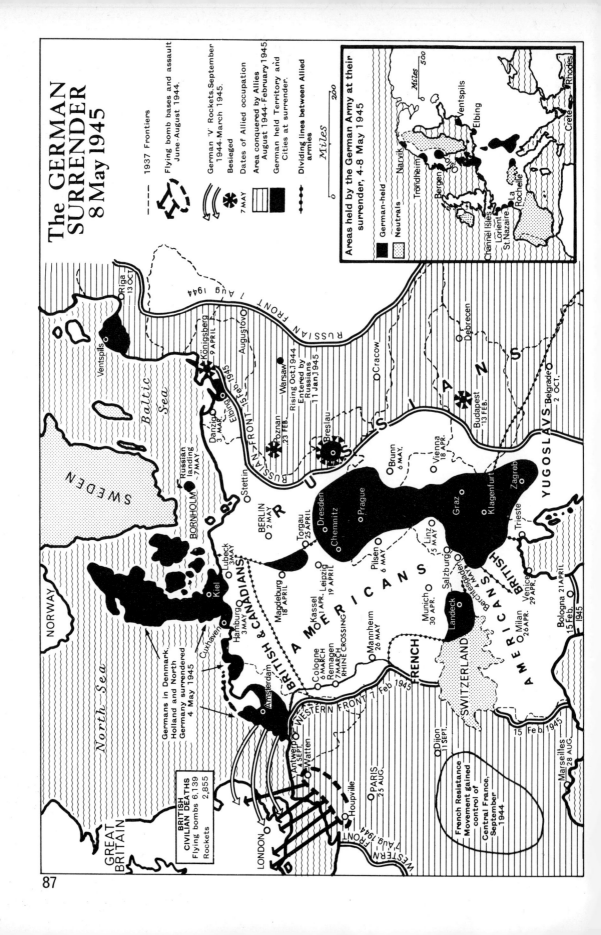

The GERMAN SURRENDER 8 May 1945

1937 Frontiers

Flying bomb bases and assault June–August 1944.

German 'V' Rockets, September 1944–March 1945.

Besieged

Dates of Allied occupation

Area conquered by Allies August 1944–February 1945

German held Territory and Cities at surrender.

Dividing lines between Allied armies

Areas held by the German Army at their surrender, 4–8 May 1945

German-held

Neutrals

Narvik

Trondheim

Bergen

Ventspils

Elbing

Channel Isles

Lorient

St. Nazaire

La Rochelle

Crete

Rhodes

Miles
0   200   500

GREAT BRITAIN

NORWAY

SWEDEN

North Sea

Baltic Sea

Riga 13 OCT

RUSSIAN FRONT 7 Aug 1944

Königsberg 9 APRIL

Augustovo

Elbing 15 Feb. 1945

Danzig 3 MAR.

Warsaw Rising Oct.1944 Entered by Russians 11 Jan.1945

Poznan 23 FEB.

RUSSIAN FRONT

Cracow

Breslau

BALKANS

Debrecen

Budapest 13 FEB.

Vienna 18 APR.

Brunn 6 MAY.

Graz

Klagenfurt

Zagreb

Trieste

YUGOSLAVS Belgrade 2 OCT.

Ventspils

Russian landing 7 MAY

BORNHOLM Russian landing 7 MAY

Stettin

BERLIN 2 MAY

Torgau 25 April

Dresden

Chemnitz

Prague

Pilsen 6 MAY

Linz 5 MAY

Salzburg

Landeck

Munich 30 APR.

Berchtesgaden 4 MAY

SWITZERLAND

AMERICANS

BRITISH

Venice 29 APR.

Milan 26 APR.

Bologna 21 APRIL 1945

15 Feb. 1945

Kiel

Lübeck

Hamburg 3 MAY

Cuxhaven

Germans in Denmark, Holland and North Germany surrendered 4 May 1945

BRITISH & CANADIANS

AMERICANS

Magdeburg 18 APRIL

Kassel

Leipzig 19 APRIL

Mannheim 26 MAY

Cologne 6 MARCH

Remagen 7 MARCH RHINE CROSSING

FRENCH

WESTERN FRONT 7 Feb 1945

Amsterdam

Antwerp 4 SEPT.

Watten

Houpville

PARIS 25 AUG.

Dijon 11 SEPT.

French Resistance Movement gained control of Central France, September 1944

15 Feb 1945

Marseilles 28 AUG.

WESTERN FRONT 7 Aug 1944

LONDON

BRITISH CIVILIAN DEATHS
Flying bombs 6,139
Rockets 2,855

87

The RETURN of GERMANS to GERMANY During the War 1939-1944

North Sea

DENMARK

S.W.E.D.E.N

Baltic Sea

ESTONIA

LATVIA

LITHUANIA

78,000

57,000

Berlin

GERMANY

350,000

33,000

30,000

POLAND

R U S S I A

Miles
0   200

- - - 1939 Boundaries
▬▬ Boundary of the German Reich 1940
◀━ Returning Germans (total 882,000)
▦ Major resettlement area 1940-44

Protectorate

SLOVAKIA

96,000

4000

SWITZ

Austria

HUNGARY

118,000

80,000

ITALY

36,000

Adriatic Sea

YUGOSLAVIA

RUMANIA

Black Sea

88

The EXPULSION of GERMANS from CENTRAL EUROPE 1945-1947

North Sea

DENMARK

S.W.E.D.E.N

Baltic Sea

2,000,000

400,000

175,000

Berlin

R U S S I A

- - - 1945 Boundaries
▬▬ The Eastern boundary of Germany 1940
▬▬ The Boundary of Germany 1945
▦ Major German resettlement area 1940-44
◀━ Expelled Germans (total 9,470,000)
≡ The Iron Curtain dividing West & East Germany.

2,500,000

POLAND

W E S T G E R M A N Y

3,500,000

CZECHOSLOVAKIA

Miles
0   200

400,000

SWITZ

AUSTRIA

50,000

ITALIANS

200,000

HUNGARY

140,000
TRIESTE

ITALY

RUMANIA

Adriatic Sea

250,000

YUGOSLAVIA

Black Sea

89

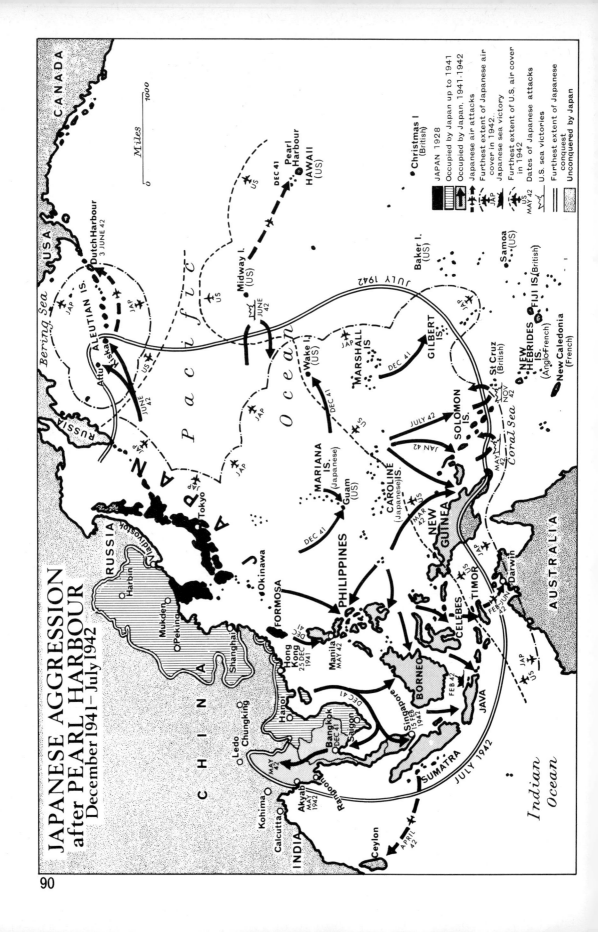

JAPANESE AGGRESSION after PEARL HARBOUR
December 1941– July 1942

Legend:
- JAPAN 1928
- Occupied by Japan up to 1941
- Occupied by Japan, 1941–1942
- Japanese air attacks
- Furthest extent of Japanese air cover in 1942.
- Japanese sea victory
- Furthest extent of U.S. air cover in 1942
- Dates of Japanese attacks
- U.S. sea victories
- Furthest extent of Japanese conquest
- Unconquered by Japan

CANADA

USA

Bering Sea

RUSSIA

Pacific Ocean

Dutch Harbour 3 JUNE 42

ALEUTIAN IS.

Attu
Kiska
JUNE 42

JAP

Pearl Harbour
HAWAII (US)
DEC 41

US

Midway I. (US)
JUNE 42

US

JULY 1942

Baker I. (US)

Samoa (US)

Wake I. (US)
DEC 41

JAP

US

GILBERT IS.
DEC 41

St Cruz (British)
NOV 42

NEW HEBRIDES (Anglo-French)

FIJI IS (British)

New Caledonia (French)

MARSHALL IS.
JAP

SOLOMON IS.
JULY 42
JAN 42
MAY 42

Coral Sea

Christmas I (British) JAPAN 1928

MARIANA IS. (Japanese)
Guam (US)

CAROLINE (Japanese) IS.
MAR 42

NEW GUINEA
JAP

Tokyo

RUSSIA
Vladivostok
Harbin
Mukden
Peking
Shanghai

CHINA

Ledo
Chungking

Kohima

Calcutta

INDIA

Akyab MAY 1942

Rangoon

Bangkok DEC 41

Hanoi
Saigon
MAY 42

Hong Kong 25 DEC 1941
DEC 41

Okinawa

FORMOSA

PHILIPPINES

Manila MAY 42
DEC 41

Singapore 15 FEB 1942

BORNEO
FEB 42

SUMATRA

JAVA
JULY 1942

CELEBES

TIMOR
FEB 42
JUNE 42

Darwin

AUSTRALIA

Indian Ocean

Ceylon
APRIL 42

Miles
0   1000

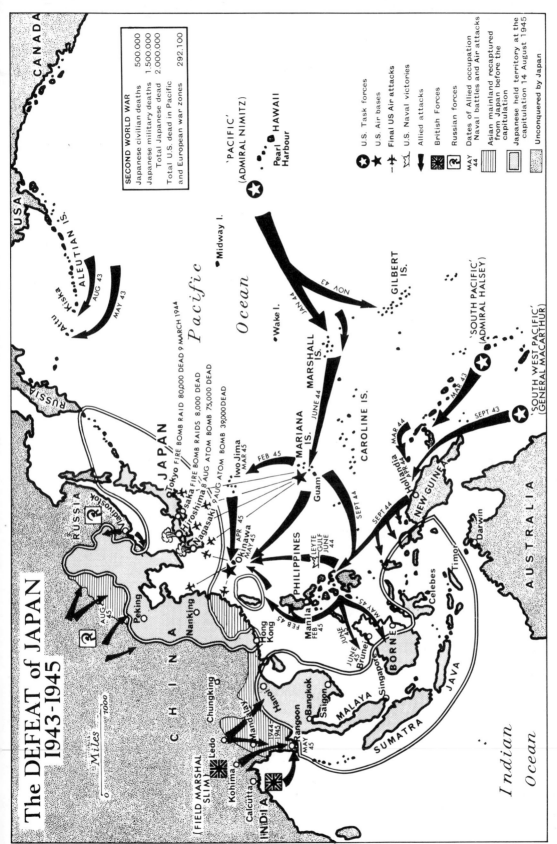

The DEFEAT of JAPAN 1943-1945

SECOND WORLD WAR

Japanese civilian deaths	500,000
Japanese military deaths	1,500,000
Total Japanese dead	2,000,000
Total U.S. dead in Pacific and European war zones	292,100

★ U.S. Task forces
★ U.S. Air bases
--✈-- Final US Air attacks
⟿ U.S. Naval victories
⬇ Allied attacks
✳ British Forces
℞ Russian Forces

MAY 44 Dates of Allied occupation
         Naval battles and Air attacks
Asian mainland recaptured from Japan before the capitulation
Japanese held territory at the capitulation 14 August 1945
Unconquered by Japan

CANADA

USA

U.S.S.R.

ALEUTIAN IS.
Kiska Attu
AUG 43
MAY 43

Midway I.

Pacific Ocean

'PACIFIC' (ADMIRAL NIMITZ)

Pearl HAWAII Harbour

Wake I.

GILBERT IS.
NOV 43
JAN 44

MARSHALL IS.
JUNE 44

MARIANA IS.

CAROLINE IS.

'SOUTH PACIFIC' (ADMIRAL HALSEY)
MAR 43

'SOUTH WEST PACIFIC' (GENERAL MACARTHUR)
SEPT 43

MAR 44
APR 44
Hollandia

NEW GUINEA

SEPT 44
SEPT 44

JAPAN
Tokyo FIRE BOMB RAID 80,000 DEAD 9 MARCH 1944
Osaka FIRE BOMB RAIDS 8,000 DEAD
Hiroshima 8 AUG ATOM BOMB 75,000 DEAD
Nagasaki 9 AUG ATOM BOMB 39,000 DEAD

Iwo Jima
FEB 45
MAR 45
Guam

Okinawa
APR 45
MAY 45

RUSSIA
Vladivostok
℞

Peking
Nanking

CHINA

PHILIPPINES
LEYTE GULF JUNE 44
Manila FEB 45
FEB 45

Hong Kong

JUNE 45
Brunei
BORNEO
MAY 45

Celebes
Timor
Darwin

AUSTRALIA

INDIA
Calcutta
Kohima
Ledo Chungking
(FIELD MARSHAL SLIM)
Mandalay
1944/1945
Rangoon
MAY 45

Bangkok
Saigon

MALAYA
Singapore
SUMATRA
JAVA

Indian Ocean

AUG 45
℞

Miles 1000

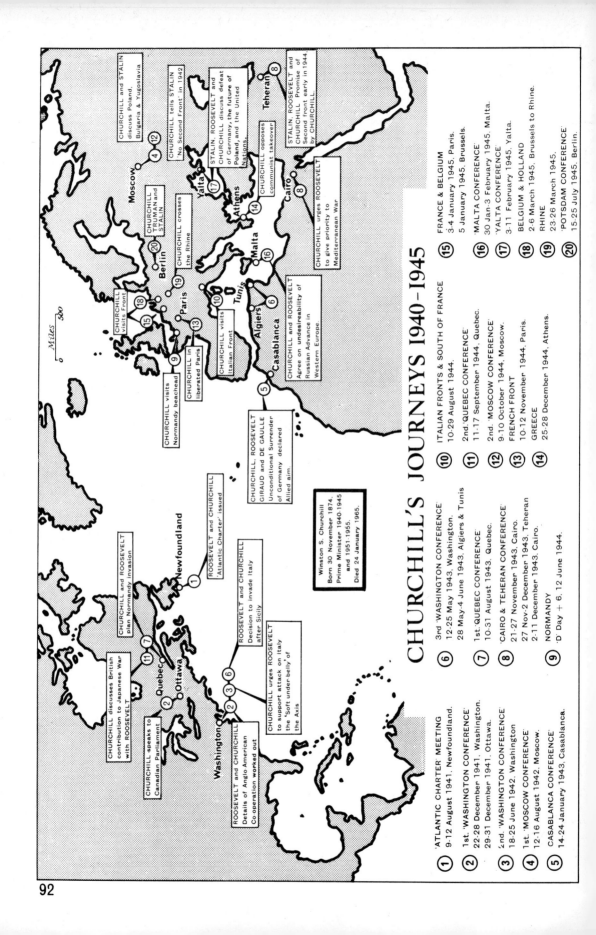

CHURCHILL'S JOURNEYS 1940–1945

Miles
0   500

Winston S. Churchill
Born 30 November 1874.
Prime Minister 1940–1945
and 1951–1955.
Died 24 January 1965.

CHURCHILL and STALIN discuss Poland, Bulgaria & Yugoslavia.

CHURCHILL tells STALIN 'No Second Front' in 1942.

STALIN, ROOSEVELT and CHURCHILL discuss defeat of Germany, the future of Poland, and the United Nations.

CHURCHILL opposes communist takeover.

STALIN, ROOSEVELT and CHURCHILL Promise of Second front early in 1944, by CHURCHILL.

CHURCHILL urges ROOSEVELT to give priority to Mediterranean War.

CHURCHILL crosses the Rhine.

CHURCHILL, TRUMAN and STALIN.

CHURCHILL in liberated Paris.

CHURCHILL visits Italian Front.

CHURCHILL and ROOSEVELT Agree on undesireability of Russian Advance in Western Europe.

CHURCHILL, ROOSEVELT, GIRAUD and DE GAULLE Unconditional Surrender of Germany declared Allied aim.

CHURCHILL visits Normandy beachead.

CHURCHILL and ROOSEVELT plan Normandy invasion.

ROOSEVELT and CHURCHILL 'Atlantic Charter' issued.

CHURCHILL discusses British contribution to Japanese War with ROOSEVELT.

CHURCHILL speaks to Canadian Parliament.

ROOSEVELT and CHURCHILL Details of Anglo American Co operation worked out.

CHURCHILL urges ROOSEVELT to support attack on Italy the 'Soft under belly' of the Axis.

ROOSEVELT and CHURCHILL Decision to invade Italy after Sicily.

Moscow
Teheran
Yalta
Athens
Cairo
Berlin
Paris
Malta
Tunis
Algiers
Casablanca
Newfoundland
Quebec
Ottawa
Washington

① 'ATLANTIC CHARTER' MEETING
   9-12 August 1941. Newfoundland.

② 1st 'WASHINGTON CONFERENCE'
   22-28 December 1941. Washington.
   29-31 December 1941. Ottawa.

③ 2nd. 'WASHINGTON CONFERENCE'
   18-25 June 1942. Washington

④ 1st 'MOSCOW CONFERENCE'
   12-16 August 1942. Moscow.

⑤ CASABLANCA CONFERENCE'
   14-24 January 1943. Casablanca.

⑥ 3rd 'WASHINGTON CONFERENCE'
   12-25 May 1943. Washington.
   28 May-4 June 1943. Algiers & Tunis.

⑦ 1st 'QUEBEC CONFERENCE'
   10-31 August 1943. Quebec.

⑧ 'CAIRO & TEHERAN CONFERENCE'
   21-27 November 1943. Cairo.
   27 Nov-2 December 1943. Teheran
   2-11 December 1943. Cairo.

⑨ NORMANDY
   'D' Day + 6. 12 June 1944.

⑩ ITALIAN FRONTS & SOUTH OF FRANCE
   10-29 August 1944.

⑪ 2nd.'QUEBEC CONFERENCE'
   11-17 September 1944. Quebec.

⑫ 2nd. 'MOSCOW CONFERENCE'
   9-10 October 1944. Moscow.

⑬ FRENCH FRONT
   10-12 November 1944. Paris.

⑭ GREECE
   25-28 December 1944. Athens.

⑮ FRANCE & BELGIUM
   3-4 January 1945. Paris.
   5 January 1945. Brussels.

⑯ 'MALTA CONFERENCE'
   30 Jan-3 February 1945. Malta.

⑰ 'YALTA CONFERENCE'
   3-11 February 1945. Yalta.

⑱ BELGIUM & HOLLAND
   2-6 March 1945. Brussels to Rhine.

⑲ RHINE
   23-26 March 1945.

⑳ 'POTSDAM CONFERENCE'
   15-25 July 1945. Berlin.

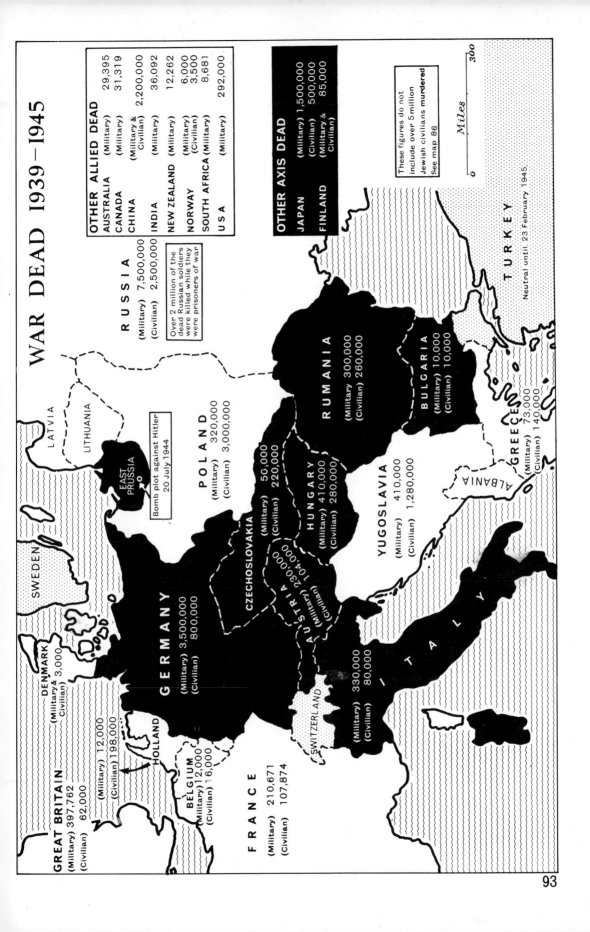

EUROPE 1945-1948

- - - - 1937 Frontiers
Allied Control Zones of Germany & Austria
Ceded to Russia by Britain & America
Cities divided into 4 Occupation Zones
Annexed by Russia in 1945
States which became Communist between 1945 & 1948
Yugoslav gains from Italy 1945
The 'Iron Curtain' from 1948
Germany since 1945

FINLAND

Viborg
Leningrad

SWEDEN

ESTONIA
Pskov

Baltic Sea

DENMARK

LATVIA
Riga

LITHUANIA
Memel
Danzig
Königsberg
EAST PRUSSIA
annexed by Poland
Vilna
Minsk

American
Bremen
HOLLAND
Szczecin (Stettin)
annexed by Poland
Poznan
Warsaw
Pinsk
R U S S I A

British
Berlin
Russian
P O L A N D

American
Erfurt
Wroclaw (Breslau)
Lvov

FRANCE
French
Prague
C Z E C H O S L O V A K I A
Cracow
Czernowitz

Nuremberg
(Trials 1945-46)
American
USA
AUSTRIA
Vienna
Russian
Uzhgorod
Kishinev

SWITZERLAND
French
French
British
Budapest
H U N G A R Y
R U M A N I A
Monarchy abolished 1947

Trieste
BRITISH & US OCCUPATION 1945-1955
Pola

I T A L Y
Monarchy abolished after June 1946 Plebiscite

Y U G O S L A V I A
Monarchy abolished 1945
Belgrade
Bucharest

Adriatic sea

A L B A N I A
Monarchy abolished 1946

B U L G A R I A
Sofia
Monarchy abolished 1946

Communist activity 1946-1949
G R E E C E
Monarchy restored after September 1946 Plebiscite
Aegean

T U R K E Y

Miles
5   100

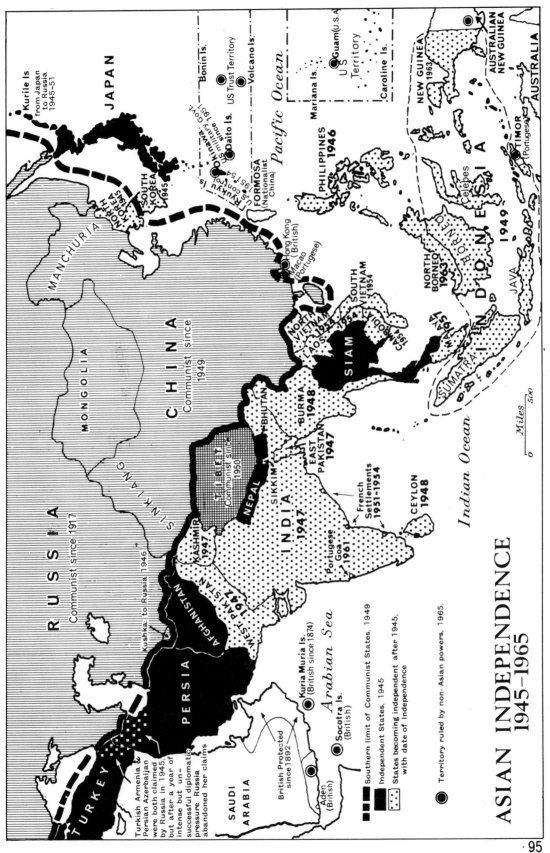

ASIAN INDEPENDENCE 1945–1965

Kurile Is from Japan to Russia 1945–51

JAPAN

MANCHURIA

NORTH KOREA 1945
SOUTH KOREA 1945

Bonin Is.
US Trust Territory
Daito Is.
Volcano Is.

RYUKYU Is U.S. control 1951–54
Okinawa US military Govt. 1951

Guam (U.S.A)

US Territory

Mariana Is.
Caroline Is.

NEW GUINEA 1963

AUSTRALIAN NEW GUINEA

Pacific Ocean

FORMOSA Nationalist China

RUSSIA Communist since 1917

MONGOLIA

SINKIANG

CHINA Communist since 1949

Hong Kong (British)
Macao (Portugese)

NORTH VIETNAM 1954
LAOS 1954
SOUTH VIETNAM 1954
CAMBODIA 1954

SIAM

MALAYA 1957

NORTH BORNEO 1963

INDONESIA 1949

Celebes

JAVA

SUMATRA

BORNEO

TIMOR (Portugese)

AUSTRALIA

TIBET Communist since 1950

NEPAL
SIKKIM
BHUTAN

BURMA 1948

EAST PAKISTAN 1947

INDIA 1947

KASHMIR 1947

AFGHANISTAN

WEST PAKISTAN 1947

Kushka. to Russia 1946

PERSIA

TURKEY

Turkish Armenia & Persian Azerbaijan were both claimed by Russia in 1945, but after a year of intense but un-successful diplomatic pressure Russia abandoned her claims

SAUDI ARABIA

Aden (British)
British Protected since 1892

Socotra Is. (British)

Kuria Muria Is. (British since 1874)

Arabian Sea

French Settlements 1951–1954

Portugese Goa 1961

CEYLON 1948

Indian Ocean

Miles
0   500

Southern limit of Communist States, 1949

Independent States, 1945

States becoming independent after 1945, with date of Independence

Territory ruled by non-Asian powers, 1965.

95

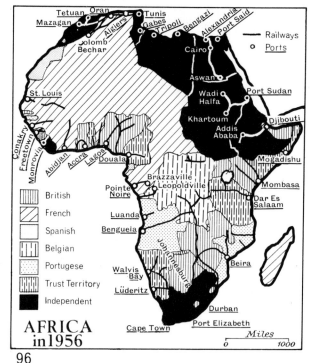

AFRICA in 1956

Legend: British, French, Spanish, Belgian, Portugese, Trust Territory, Independent — Railways, Ports

MOROCCO 1956 12½ million
IFNI SPANISH 50,000
RIO DE ORO SPANISH 24,000
MAURITANIA 1960 800,000
SENEGAL 1960 3½ million
GAMBIA 1965 300,000
GUINEA PORTUGESE ½ million
GUINEA 1958 3 million
SIERRE LEONE 1961 2½ million
LIBERIA 1847 1 million
UPPER VOLTA 1960 4½ million
IVO COA 19 3½ m
GHAN 195 7 mill

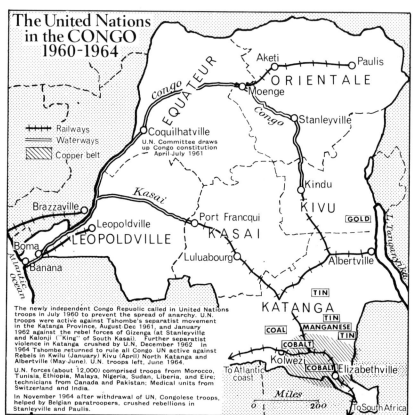

The United Nations in the CONGO 1960-1964

Railways
Waterways
Copper belt

U.N. Committee draws up Congo constitution April-July 1961

The newly independent Congo Repuolic called in United Nations troops in July 1960 to prevent the spread of anarchy. U.N. troops were active against Tshombe's separatist movement in the Katanga Province, August-Dec 1961, and January 1962 against the rebel forces of Gizenga (at Stanleyville and Kalonji ("King" of South Kasai). Further separatist violence in Katanga crushed by U.N. December 1962 In 1964 Tshombe returned to rule all Congo UN active against Rebels in Kwilu (January) Kivu (April) North Katanga and Albertville (May-June). U.N. troops left, June 1964.

U.N. forces (about 12,000) comprised troops from Morocco, Tunisia, Ethiopia, Malaya, Nigeria, Sudan, Liberia, and Eire; technicians from Canada and Pakistan; Medical units from Switzerland and India.

In November 1964 after withdrawal of UN, Congolese troops, helped by Belgian paratroopers, crushed rebellions in Stanleyville and Paulis.

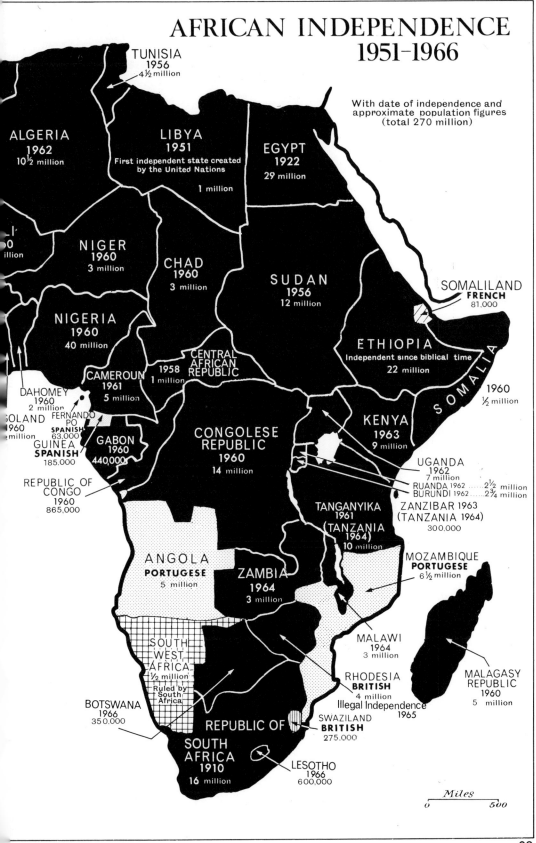

AFRICAN INDEPENDENCE
1951-1966

With date of independence and
approximate population figures
(total 270 million)

TUNISIA
1956
4½ million

ALGERIA
1962
10½ million

LIBYA
1951
First independent state created
by the United Nations
1 million

EGYPT
1922
29 million

NIGER
1960
3 million

CHAD
1960
3 million

SUDAN
1956
12 million

SOMALILAND
FRENCH
81,000

NIGERIA
1960
40 million

CENTRAL
AFRICAN
REPUBLIC
1958
1 million

ETHIOPIA
Independent since biblical time
22 million

CAMEROUN
1961
5 million

DAHOMEY
1960
2 million

FERNANDO
PO
SPANISH
63,000

KENYA
1963
9 million

1960
½ million

GOLAND
1960
million

GUINEA
SPANISH
185,000

GABON
1960
440,000

CONGOLESE
REPUBLIC
1960
14 million

UGANDA
1962
7 million

RUANDA 1962 ......2½ million
BURUNDI 1962 ......2¾ million

ZANZIBAR 1963
(TANZANIA 1964)
300,000

REPUBLIC OF
CONGO
1960
865,000

TANGANYIKA
1961
(TANZANIA
1964)
10 million

MOZAMBIQUE
PORTUGESE
6½ million

ANGOLA
PORTUGESE
5 million

ZAMBIA
1964
3 million

MALAWI
1964
3 million

MALAGASY
REPUBLIC
1960
5 million

SOUTH
WEST
AFRICA
½ million
Ruled by
South
Africa

RHODESIA
BRITISH
4 million
Illegal Independence
1965

SWAZILAND
BRITISH
275,000

BOTSWANA
1966
350,000

REPUBLIC OF
SOUTH
AFRICA
1910
16 million

LESOTHO
1966
600,000

SOMALIA

Miles
0   500

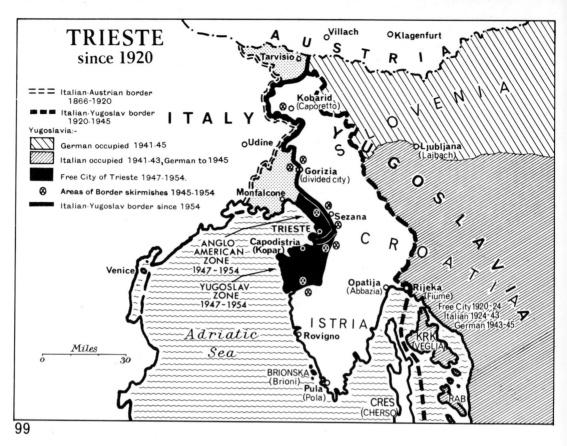

TRIESTE
since 1920

=== Italian-Austrian border
1866-1920

▬▬▬ Italian-Yugoslav border
1920-1945

Yugoslavia:-

▨ German occupied 1941-45

▧ Italian occupied 1941-43, German to 1945

■ Free City of Trieste 1947-1954.

⊗ Areas of Border skirmishes 1945-1954

▬ Italian-Yugoslav border since 1954

A U S T R I A

°Villach   °Klagenfurt

Tarvisio°

I T A L Y

Y U G O S L A V I A

Kobarid°
(Caporetto) ⊗

°Udine

°Ljubljana
(Laibach)

C R O A T I A

⊗ Gorizia
(divided city)

Monfalcone°

⊗ Sezana

TRIESTE
Capodistria
(Kopar)

ANGLO-
AMERICAN-
ZONE
1947-1954

YUGOSLAV
ZONE
1947-1954

Venice°

Opatija
(Abbazia)   ⊗ Rijeka
(Fiume)
Free City 1920-24
Italian 1924-43
German 1943-45

I S T R I A

KRK
(VEGLIA)

°Rovigno

*Adriatic
Sea*

Miles
0   30

BRIONSKA
(Brioni)
Pula
(Pola)

CRES
(CHERSO)

RAB

99

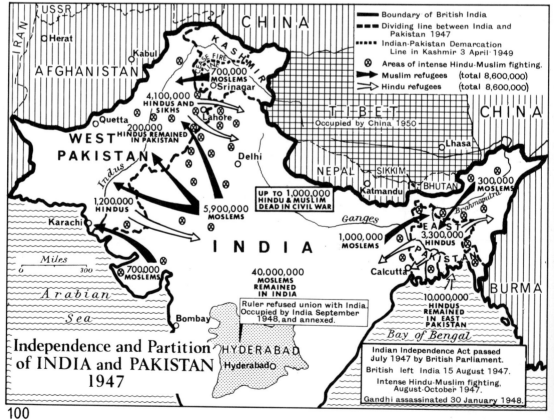

USSR

IRAN

C H I N A

°Herat

KASHMIR

Kabul°

CEASE FIRE LINE

700,000
MOSLEMS
Srinagar°

A F G H A N I S T A N

4,100,000
HINDUS AND
SIKHS

°Quetta   ⊗   ⊗ Lahore

T I B E T
Occupied by China 1950

C H I N A

200,000
HINDUS REMAINED
IN PAKISTAN

WEST
PAKISTAN

°Delhi

Lhasa°

Indus

N E P A L

SIKKIM

BHUTAN

300,000
MOSLEMS

Katmandu°

1,200,000
HINDUS

5,900,000
MOSLEMS

UP TO 1,000,000
HINDU & MUSLIM
DEAD IN CIVIL WAR

Ganges

Brahmaputra

E A S T

Karachi°

1,000,000
MOSLEMS

3,300,000
HINDUS

P A K I S T A N

I N D I A

Calcutta°

Miles
0   300

700,000
MOSLEMS

40,000,000
MOSLEMS
REMAINED
IN INDIA

BURMA

10,000,000
HINDUS
REMAINED
IN EAST
PAKISTAN

*Arabian
Sea*

Bombay°

Ruler refused union with India.
Occupied by India September
1948, and annexed.

Bay of Bengal

Independence and Partition
of INDIA and PAKISTAN
1947

HYDERABAD

Hyderabad°

▬▬ Boundary of British India

▬▬▬ Dividing line between India and
Pakistan 1947

▪▪▪▪ Indian-Pakistan Demarcation
Line in Kashmir 3 April 1949

⊗ Areas of intense Hindu-Muslim fighting.

➤ Muslim refugees (total 8,600,000)

⇨ Hindu refugees (total 8,600,000)

Indian Independence Act passed
July 1947 by British Parliament.
British left India 15 August 1947.
Intense Hindu-Muslim fighting,
August-October 1947.
Gandhi assassinated 30 January 1948.

100

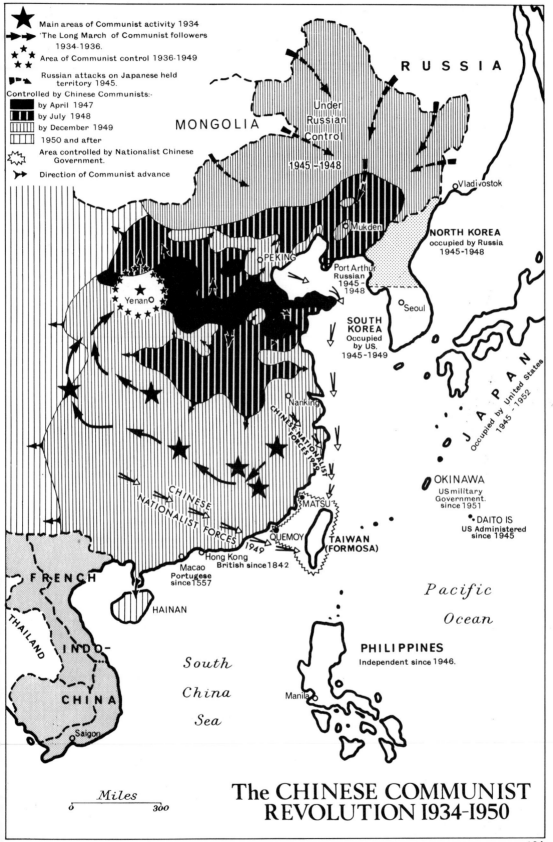

Legend:

- ★ Main areas of Communist activity 1934
- ➡ 'The Long March' of Communist followers 1934-1936.
- ★★★ Area of Communist control 1936-1949
- ★★
- ◤◤◤ Russian attacks on Japanese held territory 1945.

Controlled by Chinese Communists:-
- ▰ by April 1947
- ▥ by July 1948
- ▦ by December 1949
- ▤ 1950 and after
- ⟋⟍ Area controlled by Nationalist Chinese Government.
- ➤ Direction of Communist advance

RUSSIA

MONGOLIA

Under Russian Control 1945-1948

Vladivostok

Mukden

NORTH KOREA occupied by Russia 1945-1948

PEKING

Port Arthur Russian 1945-1948

Yenan

Seoul

SOUTH KOREA Occupied by U.S. 1945-1949

Nanking

JAPAN Occupied by United States 1945-1952

CHINESE NATIONALIST FORCES 1949

OKINAWA US military Government. since 1951

DAITO IS US Administered since 1945

MATSU

QUEMOY

TAIWAN (FORMOSA)

CHINESE NATIONALIST FORCES 1949

Hong Kong British since 1842

Macao Portugese since 1557

HAINAN

Pacific Ocean

FRENCH

THAILAND

INDO-

CHINA

South China Sea

PHILIPPINES Independent since 1946.

Manila

Saigon

Miles
0   300

The CHINESE COMMUNIST REVOLUTION 1934-1950

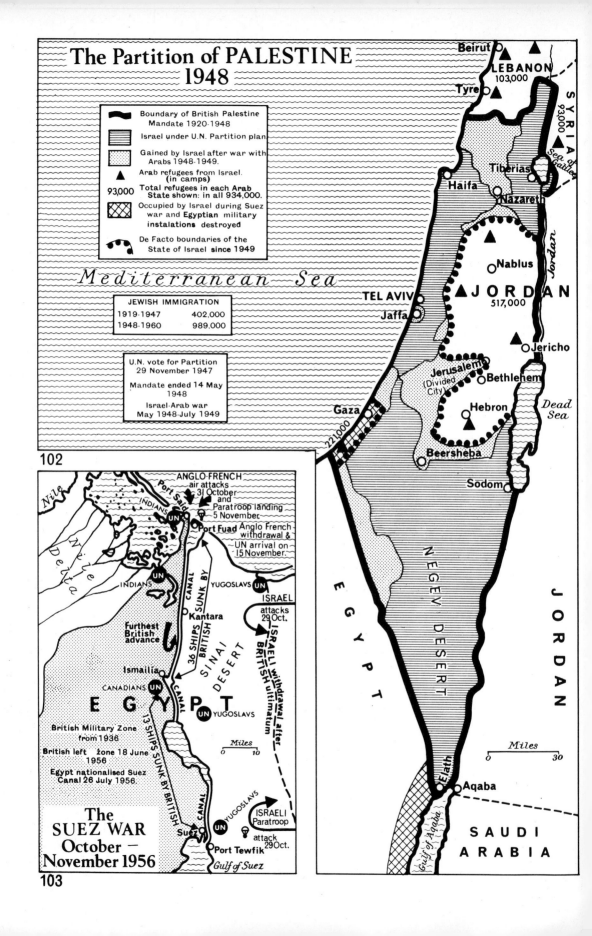

The Partition of PALESTINE 1948

Legend:
- Boundary of British Palestine Mandate 1920-1948
- Israel under U.N. Partition plan
- Gained by Israel after war with Arabs 1948-1949.
- ▲ Arab refugees from Israel. (in camps)
- 93,000 Total refugees in each Arab State shown: in all 934,000.
- Occupied by Israel during Suez war and **Egyptian** military installations destroyed
- De Facto boundaries of the State of Israel **since** 1949

Mediterranean Sea

JEWISH IMMIGRATION
1919-1947	402,000
1948-1960	989,000

U.N. vote for Partition 29 November 1947

Mandate ended 14 May 1948

Israel-Arab war May 1948-July 1949

Beirut

LEBANON 103,000

Tyre

SYRIA 93,000

Sea of Galilee

Tiberias

Haifa

Nazareth

Nablus

JORDAN 517,000

Jordan

TEL AVIV

Jaffa

Jericho

Jerusalem (Divided City)

Bethlehem

Dead Sea

Gaza 221,000

Hebron

Beersheba

Sodom

NEGEV DESERT

EGYPT

JORDAN

Elath

Aqaba

Gulf of Aqaba

SAUDI ARABIA

Miles 0 — 30

102

The SUEZ WAR October — November 1956

Nile

Nile Delta

Port Said

INDIANS

ANGLO-FRENCH air attacks 31 October and Paratroop landing 5 November.

UN

Port Fuad

Anglo French withdrawal & UN arrival on 15 November.

INDIANS UN

UN YUGOSLAVS

ISRAEL attacks 29 Oct.

Kantara

CANAL SUNK BY

36 SHIPS BRITISH

SINAI DESERT

ISRAELI withdrawal after BRITISH ultimatum

Furthest British advance

Ismailia

CANADIANS UN

CANAL

13 SHIPS SUNK BY BRITISH

EGYPT

UN YUGOSLAVS

British Military Zone from 1936

British left zone 18 June 1956

Egypt nationalised Suez Canal 26 July 1956.

Miles 0 — 10

CANAL

Suez UN

YUGOSLAVS

ISRAELI Paratroop attack 29 Oct.

Port Tewfik

Gulf of Suez

103

UNITED STATES activity in the CARIBBEAN 1895-1939

UNITED STATES

FLORIDA

Gulf of Mexico

Atlantic Ocean

Bahamas (British)

Vera Cruz (Seized 1914)

M E X I C O

CUBA
(Occupied 1898-1902.
After war with Spain)

DOMINICAN REPUBLIC
(Occupied 1916-1924)

Virgin Islands (Purchased from Denmark 1916)

Guantanamo US base since 1898

BRITISH HONDURAS

Jamaica (British)

HAITI (Occupied 1914-1934)

PUERTO RICO
(Annexed 1898. After war with Spain)

Swan Island (USA)

Caribbean Sea

GUATEMALA

HONDURAS

EL SALVADOR

NICARAGUA
(Occupied 1909-10, 1912-25, 1926-39)

Pacific Ocean

COSTA RICA

P A N A M A

VENEZUELA

Panama Canal Zone (US Protectorate 1903-1939)

COLOMBIA

Miles

0   400

104

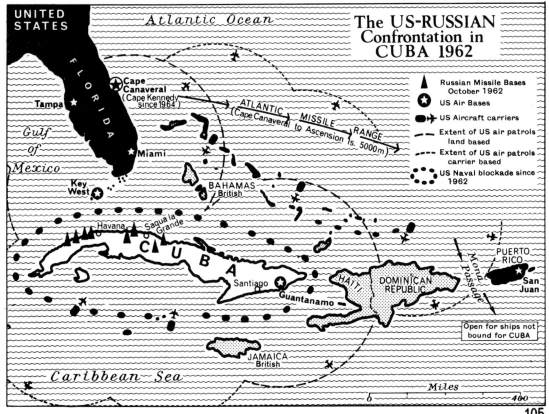

The US-RUSSIAN Confrontation in CUBA 1962

UNITED STATES

Atlantic Ocean

FLORIDA

Cape Canaveral (Cape Kennedy since 1964)

Tampa

▲ Russian Missile Bases October 1962

☆ US Air Bases

US Aircraft carriers

ATLANTIC MISSILE RANGE (Cape Canaveral to Ascension Is. 5000m)

– – – Extent of US air patrols land based

–·–·– Extent of US air patrols carrier based

Gulf of Mexico

Miami

•••• US Naval blockade since 1962

Key West

BAHAMAS British

Havana   Sagua la Grande

C U B A

PUERTO RICO

Mona Passage

San Juan

Santiago

Guantanamo

HAITI

DOMINICAN REPUBLIC

Open for ships not bound for CUBA

JAMAICA British

Caribbean Sea

Miles

0   400

105

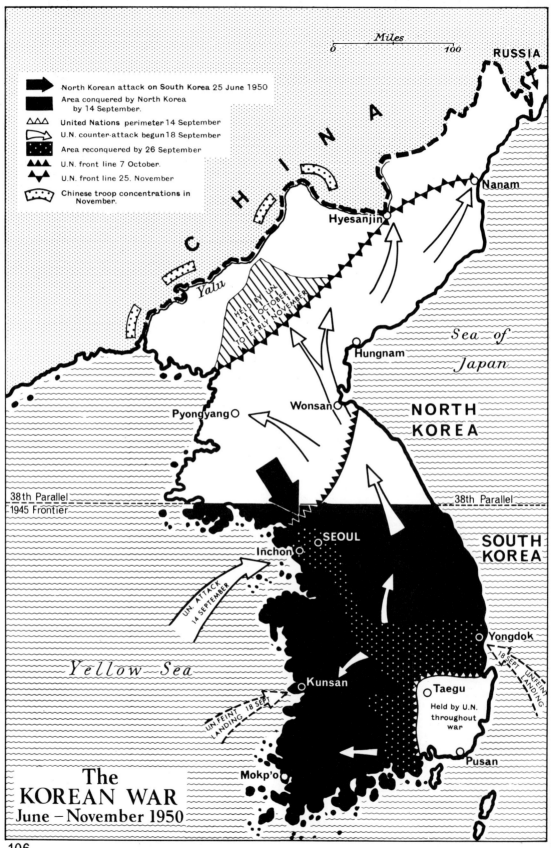

Miles

0   100

RUSSIA

➤ North Korean attack on South Korea 25 June 1950

▬ Area conquered by North Korea by 14 September.

△△△ United Nations perimeter 14 September

⟹ U.N. counter-attack begun 18 September

▨ Area reconquered by 26 September

▲▲▲ U.N. front line 7 October.

▼▼▼ U.N. front line 25. November

▨ Chinese troop concentrations in November.

C H I N A

Yalu

Nanam

Hyesanjin

HELD BY U.N.
LATE OCTOBER
TO
EARLY NOVEMBER

Sea of
Japan

Hungnam

Pyongyang

Wonsan

NORTH
KOREA

38th Parallel
1945 Frontier

38th Parallel

SEOUL

Inchon

SOUTH
KOREA

U.N. ATTACK
14 SEPTEMBER

Yellow Sea

Yongdok

18 SEPT. U.N FEINT LANDING

Kunsan

Taegu
Held by U.N.
throughout
war

U.N FEINT 18 SEP
LANDING

Pusan

Mokp'o

The
KOREAN WAR
June – November 1950

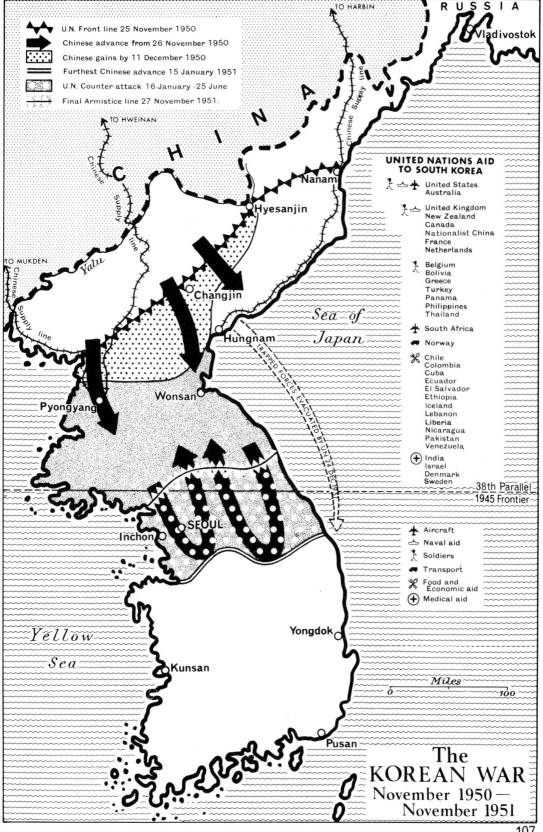

KEY

- ▲▲▲ U.N. Front line 25 November 1950
- ➡ Chinese advance from 26 November 1950
- ▨ Chinese gains by 11 December 1950
- ≡ Furthest Chinese advance 15 January 1951
- ▨ U.N. Counter-attack 16 January - 25 June
- ⇢ Final Armistice line 27 November 1951.

TO HARBIN

RUSSIA

Vladivostok

Chinese Supply line

C H I N A

TO HWEINAN

Chinese Supply line

Nanam

Hyesanjin

TO MUKDEN

Chinese Supply line

Yalu

Changjin

Hungnam

Sea of Japan

TRAPPED FORCES EVACUATED BY U.N. 24 DEC.

Pyongyang

Wonsan

UNITED NATIONS AID TO SOUTH KOREA

- United States
  Australia
- United Kingdom
  New Zealand
  Canada
  Nationalist China
  France
  Netherlands
- Belgium
  Bolivia
  Greece
  Turkey
  Panama
  Philippines
  Thailand
- South Africa
- Norway
- Chile
  Colombia
  Cuba
  Ecuador
  El Salvador
  Ethiopia
  Iceland
  Lebanon
  Liberia
  Nicaragua
  Pakistan
  Venezuela
- ⊕ India
  Israel
  Denmark
  Sweden

SEOUL

Inchon

38th Parallel
1945 Frontier

- ✈ Aircraft
- ⚓ Naval aid
- Soldiers
- Transport
- Food and Economic aid
- ⊕ Medical aid

Yellow Sea

Yongdok

Kunsan

Miles
0   100

Pusan

The
KOREAN WAR
November 1950 —
November 1951

CHINA since 1950

Miles 0 200

Tannu-Tuva. Independent 1921-1944. Annexed by Russia 1944

Russian influence 1919-1941

Independent of China 1912-1950

CHINA since 1950

Major railways

Trans-Siberian railway Moscow-Vladivostok

Non-Communist States

Areas claimed by China

First Chinese atom device tested, 16 October 1964.

RUSSIA

To Moscow
Petropavlovsk
Omsk
Tomsk
Novosibirsk
Barnaul
Krasnoyarsk
Semipalatinsk
Karaganda
Aktogay
Alma Ata
Frunze
Tashkent
Samarkand
Mery
Kashgar
Yarkand
Khotan
Kabul
Srinagar
Chusul
Demchok
WEST PAKISTAN
Karachi
TRUCIAL OMAN
IRAN
AFGHANISTAN
SINKIANG
Urumchi
Hami
Lop Nor
TIBET
Gartok
Lhasa
NEPAL
SIKKIM
BHUTAN
Calcutta
INDIA
EAST PAKISTAN
Kyzyl
Lake Baikal
Irkutsk
Chita
Ulan Ude
Ulan Bator
MONGOLIAN PEOPLES REPUBLIC
Tsining
Lanchow
CHINA
Hengyang
Wuhan
Nanking
Tezpur
Longu
BURMA
LAOS
Hanoi
NORTH VIETNAM
SIAM
Alexandrovsk
Khabarovsk
Vladivostok
Harbin
Mukden
NORTH KOREA
Pyongyang
Seoul
SOUTH KOREA
Peking
Tientsin
Shanghai
Canton
Hong Kong (British)
Macao (Portuguese)
FORMOSA (Nationalist China)
PHILIPPINES
JAPAN

108

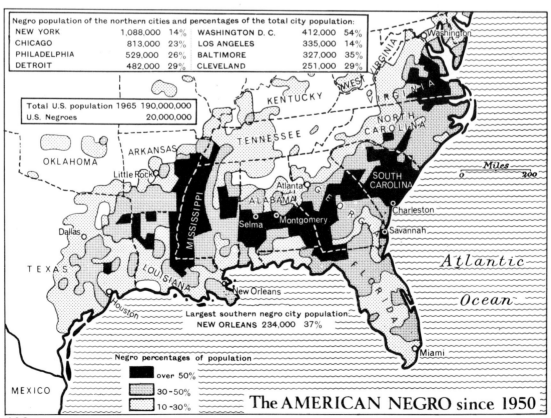

Negro population of the northern cities and percentages of the total city population:

NEW YORK	1,088,000	14%	WASHINGTON D.C.	412,000	54%
CHICAGO	813,000	23%	LOS ANGELES	335,000	14%
PHILADELPHIA	529,000	26%	BALTIMORE	327,000	35%
DETROIT	482,000	29%	CLEVELAND	251,000	29%

Total U.S. population 1965 190,000,000
U.S. Negroes 20,000,000

Miles 0 200

Washington
WEST VIRGINIA
KENTUCKY
VIRGINIA
NORTH CAROLINA
TENNESSEE
OKLAHOMA
ARKANSAS
Little Rock
SOUTH CAROLINA
Atlanta
ALABAMA
Selma
Montgomery
GEORGIA
Charleston
Savannah
Dallas
MISSISSIPPI
TEXAS
LOUISIANA
New Orleans
Houston
FLORIDA
Miami
Atlantic Ocean
MEXICO

Largest southern negro city population:
NEW ORLEANS 234,000 37%

Negro percentages of population

over 50%

30-50%

10-30%

The AMERICAN NEGRO since 1950

109

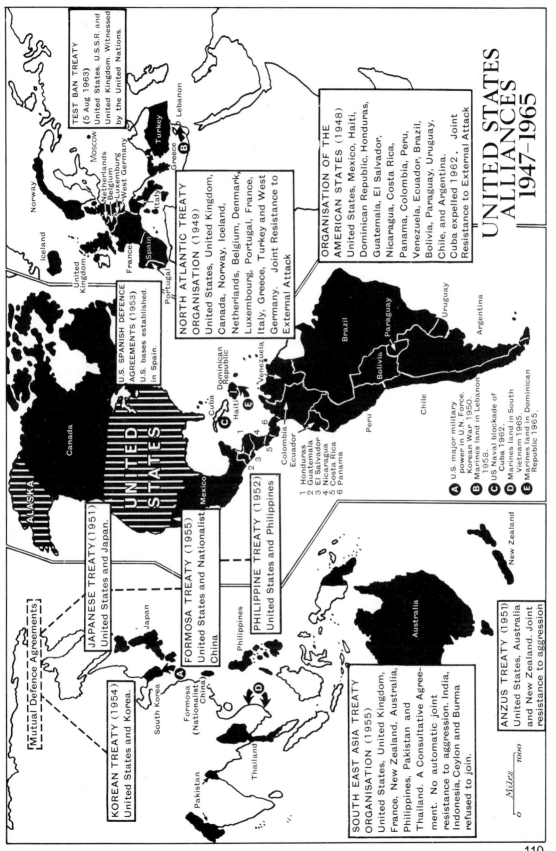

UNITED STATES
ALLIANCES
1947-1965

TEST BAN TREATY
(5 Aug 1963) United States, U.S.S.R. and United Kingdom. Witnessed by the United Nations.

NORTH ATLANTIC TREATY ORGANISATION (1949) United States, United Kingdom, Canada, Norway, Iceland, Netherlands, Belgium, Denmark, Luxembourg, Portugal, France, Italy, Greece, Turkey and West Germany. Joint Resistance to External Attack

U.S. SPANISH DEFENCE AGREEMENTS (1953) U.S. bases established in Spain.

ORGANISATION OF THE AMERICAN STATES (1948) United States, Mexico, Haiti, Dominican Republic, Honduras, Guatemala, El Salvador, Nicaragua, Costa Rica, Panama, Colombia, Peru, Venezuela, Ecuador, Brazil, Bolivia, Paraguay, Uruguay, Chile, and Argentina. Cuba expelled 1962. Joint Resistance to External Attack

Mutual Defence Agreements

JAPANESE TREATY (1951) United States and Japan.

FORMOSA TREATY (1955) United States and Nationalist China.

PHILIPPINE TREATY (1952) United States and Philippines

KOREAN TREATY (1954) United States and Korea.

SOUTH EAST ASIA TREATY ORGANISATION (1955) United States, United Kingdom, France, New Zealand, Australia, Philippines, Pakistan and Thailand. A Consultative Agreement. No automatic joint resistance to aggression. India, Indonesia, Ceylon and Burma refused to join.

ANZUS TREATY (1951) United States, Australia and New Zealand. Joint resistance to aggression

1 Honduras
2 Guatemala
3 El Salvador
4 Nicaragua
5 Costa Rica
6 Panama

Ⓐ U.S. major military power in U.N. Force. Korean War 1950.
Ⓑ Marines land in Lebanon 1958.
Ⓒ US Naval blockade of Cuba 1962.
Ⓓ Marines land in South Vietnam 1965.
Ⓔ Marines land in Dominican Republic 1965.

Miles
0   1000

110

EUROPEAN
ECONOMIC
BLOCS
since 1947

Miles
0   300

FINLAND

NORWAY
SWEDEN

DENMARK

GT BRITAIN

EIRE

HOLLAND

POLAND

RUSSIA

BELGIUM
LUXEMBURG
WEST
GERMANY
EAST
GERMANY
CZECHOSLOVAKIA

FRANCE
SWITZ
AUSTRIA
HUNGARY
RUMANIA

PORTUGAL

SPAIN

ITALY

YUGOSLAVIA
BULGARIA
ALBANIA
GREECE
TURKEY

Benelux customs Union since 1947
Comecon Mutual Economic aid since 1948
European Coal and Steel Community since 1952
European Common Market Treaty of Rome 1957
European Free Trade Association since 1958.

111

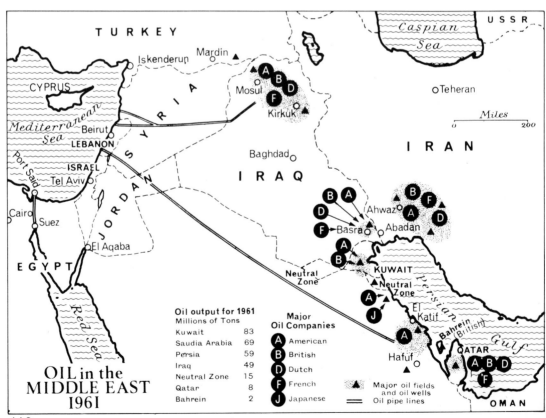

TURKEY

Iskenderun
Mardin
Mosul
Kirkuk

CYPRUS

Mediterranean Sea

Beirut
LEBANON
ISRAEL
Port Said
Tel Aviv
Cairo
Suez
El Aqaba

SYRIA

JORDAN

EGYPT

Red Sea

Caspian Sea

USSR

Teheran

IRAN

Baghdad
IRAQ

Ahwaz
Basra
Abadan

Neutral Zone

KUWAIT
Neutral Zone

El Katif
Bahrein (British)

Hafuf

QATAR

Persian Gulf

OMAN

OIL in the
MIDDLE EAST
1961

Oil output for 1961
Millions of Tons

Kuwait	83
Saudia Arabia	69
Persia	59
Iraq	49
Neutral Zone	15
Qatar	8
Bahrein	2

Major Oil Companies

A	American
B	British
D	Dutch
F	French
J	Japanese

▲ Major oil fields and oil wells
═ Oil pipe lines

112

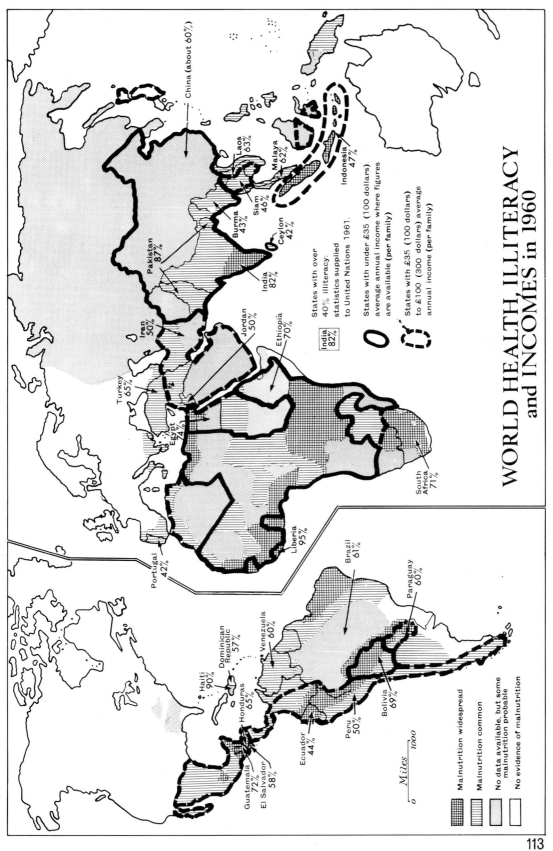

WORLD HEALTH, ILLITERACY
and INCOMES in 1960

China (about 60%)

Laos 63%
Malaya 62%
Indonesia 47%

Burma 43%
Siam 46%
Ceylon 42%

Pakistan 87%

India 82%

Iran 50%
Jordan 50%
Ethiopia 70%

Turkey 65%

Egypt 74%

South Africa 71%

Portugal 42%

Liberia 95%

Brazil 61%

Paraguay 60%

Dominican Republic 57%

Venezuela 60%

Haiti 90%

Honduras 65%

Bolivia 69%

Ecuador 44%

Peru 50%

Guatemala 72%
El Salvador 58%

States with over 40% illiteracy: statistics supplied to United Nations 1961.

India 82%

States with under £35 (100 dollars) average annual income where figures are available (per family)

States with £35 (100 dollars) to £100 (300 dollars) average annual income (per family)

Miles
0   1000

Malnutrition widespread

Malnutrition common

No data available, but some malnutrition probable

No evidence of malnutrition

113

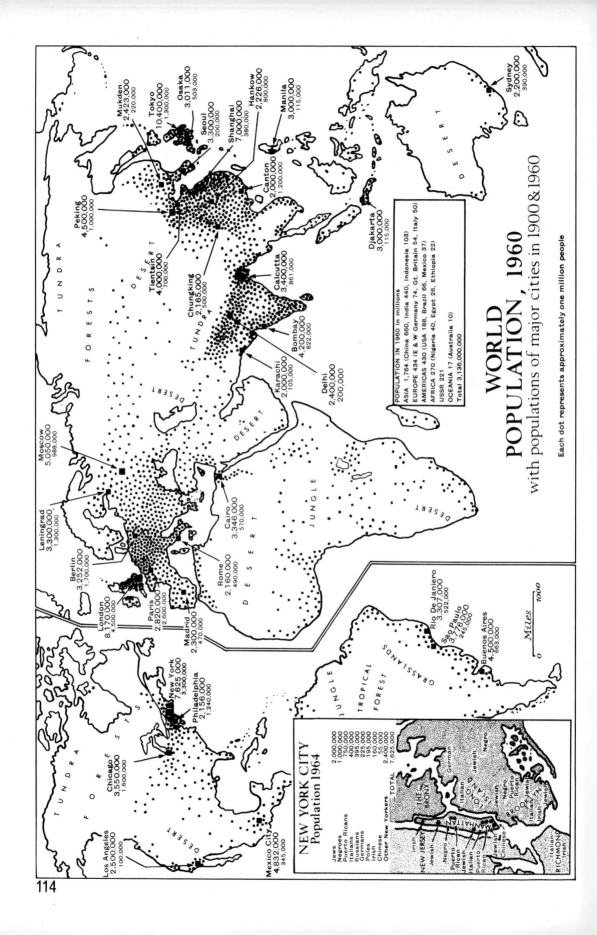

WORLD POPULATION, 1960
with populations of major cities in 1900 & 1960

Each dot represents approximately one million people

POPULATION IN 1960 in millions
ASIA 1,764 (China 660, India 440, Indonesia 103)
EUROPE 434 (E & W Germany 74, Gt. Britain 54, Italy 50)
AMERICAS 430 (USA 188, Brazil 66, Mexico 37)
AFRICA 270 (Nigeria 40, Egypt 26, Ethiopia 22)
USSR 221
OCEANIA 17 (Australia 10)
Total 3,136,000,000

Mukden 2,423,000 / 220,000
Tokyo 10,400,000 / 1,300,000
Osaka 3,011,000 / 503,000
Seoul 3,300,000 / 200,000
Shanghai 7,000,000 / 380,000
Hankow 2,226,000 / 800,000
Manila 3,000,000 / 115,000
Sydney 2,200,000 / 390,000
Peking 4,500,000 / 1,000,000
Canton 2,000,000 / 1,200,000
Tientsin 4,000,000 / 700,000
Chungking 2,165,000 / 500,000
Calcutta 3,400,000 / 861,000
Djakarta 3,000,000 / 115,000
Bombay 4,200,000 / 822,000
Karachi 2,000,000 / 105,000
Delhi 2,400,000 / 200,000
Moscow 5,050,000 / 988,000
Leningrad 3,300,000 / 1,300,000
Berlin 3,252,000 / 1,700,000
London 8,170,000 / 4,500,000
Paris 2,820,000 / 2,600,000
Madrid 2,300,000 / 470,000
Rome 2,160,000 / 490,000
Cairo 3,346,000 / 570,000
Rio De Janiero 3,307,000 / 522,000
São Paulo 3,976,000 / 245,000
Buenos Aires 4,500,000 / 663,000
New York 7,625,000 / 3,300,000
Philadelphia 2,156,000 / 1,240,000
Chicago 3,550,000 / 1,600,000
Los Angeles 2,500,000 / 100,000
Mexico City 4,832,000 / 345,000

Miles
0   1000

NEW YORK CITY
Population 1964

Jews	2,000,000
Negroes	1,000,000
Puerto Ricans	750,000
Italians	400,000
Russians	395,000
Germans	225,000
Poles	195,000
Irish	160,000
Chinese	55,000
Other New Yorkers	2,445,000
TOTAL	7,625,000

THE BRONX
Italian
Negro
Jewish
NEW JERSEY
Irish
Negro
Jewish
Puerto Rican
MANHATTAN
Italian
Puerto Rican
German
Jewish
Negro
LONG ISLAND
Italian
Jewish
BROOKLYN
Jewish
Chinese
Negro
Puerto Rican
Italian-Irish
RICHMOND
Italian
Irish

114

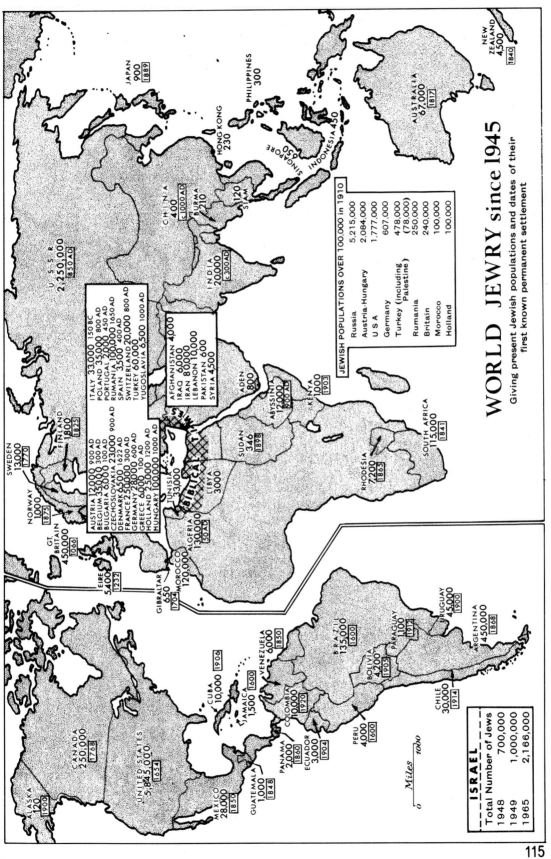

WORLD JEWRY since 1945

Giving present Jewish populations and dates of their first known permanent settlement

NEW ZEALAND 4,500 |1840|

AUSTRALIA 67,000 |1817|

JAPAN 900 |1889|

PHILIPPINES 300

HONG KONG 230

INDONESIA 450

SINGAPORE 650

CHINA 400 |c1000AD|

BURMA 210 |c300AD|

SIAM 120

U.S.S.R 2,250,000 |850AD|

INDIA 20,000 |c300AD|

JEWISH POPULATIONS OVER 100,000 in 1910	
Russia	5,215,000
Austria-Hungary	2,084,000
U S A	1,777,000
Germany	607,000
Turkey (including Palestine)	478,000 (78,000)
Rumania	250,000
Britain	240,000
Morocco	100,000
Holland	100,000

ITALY 33,000 150 BC
POLAND 35,000 800 AD
BULGARIA 8,000 100 AD
PORTUGAL 2,000 450 AD
RUMANIA 100,000 1650AD
CZECHOSLOVAKIA 23,000 900 AD
DENMARK 6,500 1622 AD
SPAIN 3,500 400 AD
FRANCE 250,000 300 AD
SWITZERLAND 20,000 800 AD
GERMANY 28,000 600 AD
TURKEY 60,000
GREECE 6,000 100 AD
YUGOSLAVIA 6,500 1000 AD
HOLLAND 25,000 1200 AD
HUNGARY 100,000 1000 AD

AUSTRIA 12,000 900 AD
BELGIUM 35,000 100 AD

AFGHANISTAN 4,000
IRAQ 6,000
IRAN 80,000
LEBANON 10,000
PAKISTAN 600
SYRIA 4,500

FINLAND 1,800 |1825|

SWEDEN 13,000 |1770|

NORWAY 1,000 |1875|

GT. BRITAIN 450,000 |1066|

EIRE 5,400 |1232|

GIBRALTAR 650 |1704|

BIBLICAL

TUNISIA 33,000

ALGERIA 130,000 |50AD|

LIBYA 3,000

MOROCCO 120,000

ADEN 800

ABYSSINIA 2,000 |200AD|

SUDAN 346 |1878|

KENYA 1,000 |1903|

RHODESIA 7,200 |1865|

SOUTH AFRICA 115,000 |1841|

ALASKA 120 |1900|

CANADA 250,000 |1768|

UNITED STATES 5,845,000 |1654|

MEXICO 28,000 |1850|

GUATEMALA 1,000 |1848|

CUBA 10,000 |1906|

JAMAICA 1,500 |1600|

PANAMA 2,000 |1860|

ECUADOR 3,000 |1904|

COLOMBIA 10,000 |1920|

VENEZUELA 6,000 |1850|

PERU 4,000 |1600|

BOLIVIA 4,200 |1905|

BRAZIL 135,000 |1600|

PARAGUAY 1,100 |1912|

URUGUAY 45,000 |1900|

ARGENTINA 450,000 |1868|

CHILE 30,000 |1914|

Miles
0   1000

ISRAEL	
Total Number of Jews	
1948	700,000
1949	1,000,000
1965	2,166,000

115

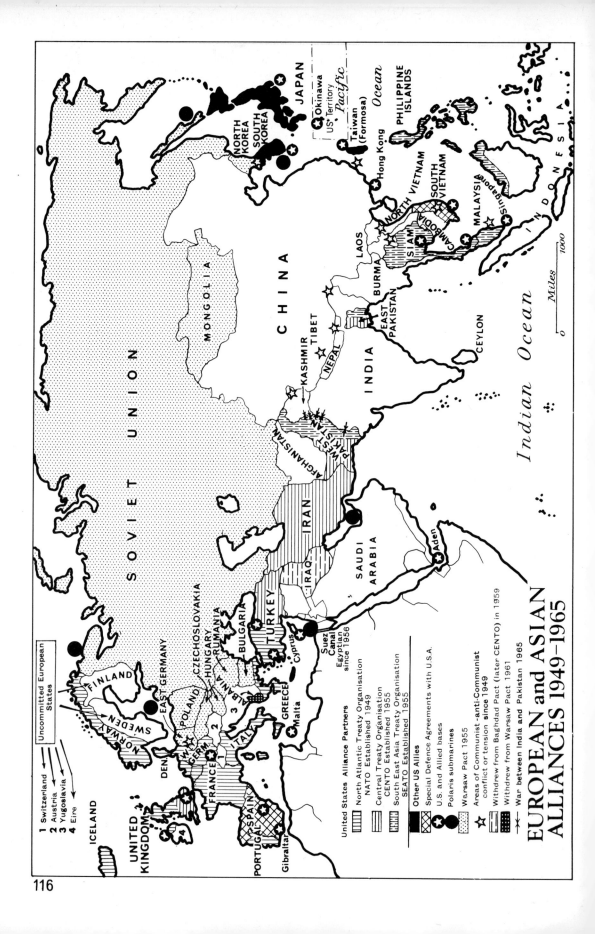

EUROPEAN and ASIAN ALLIANCES 1949-1965

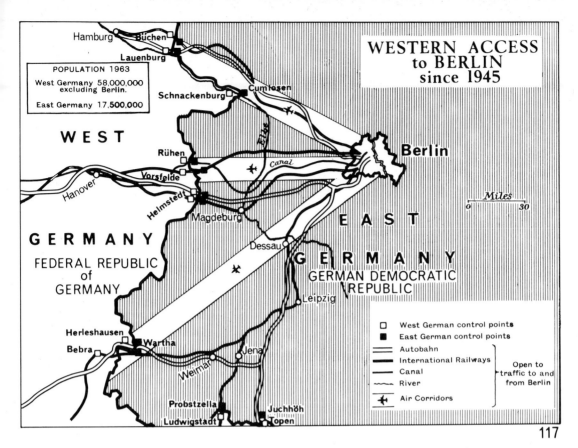

WESTERN ACCESS to BERLIN since 1945

POPULATION 1963
West Germany 58,000,000 excluding Berlin.
East Germany 17,500,000

Hamburg
Büchen
Lauenburg
Schnackenburg
Cumlosen
Berlin

WEST

Rühen
Vorsfelde
Hanover
Helmsted
Magdeburg

GERMANY

FEDERAL REPUBLIC of GERMANY

Dessau

EAST

GERMANY

GERMAN DEMOCRATIC REPUBLIC

Leipzig

Miles
0   30

Herleshausen
Bebra
Wartha
Jena
Weimar

	West German control points
□	East German control points
■	Autobahn
	International Railways
	Canal
	River
✈	Air Corridors

Open to traffic to and from Berlin

Probstzella
Juchhöh
Ludwigstadt
Topen

117

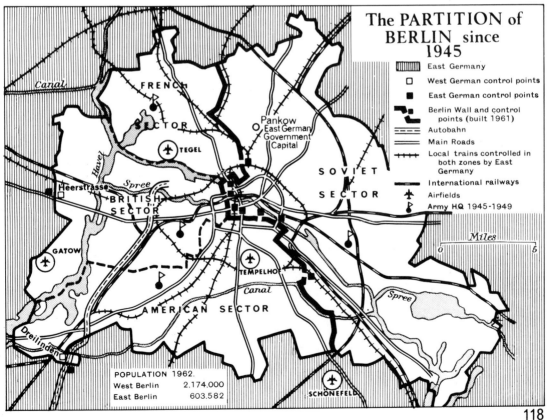

The PARTITION of BERLIN since 1945

	East Germany
□	West German control points
■	East German control points
	Berlin Wall and control points (built 1961)
	Autobahn
	Main Roads
	Local trains controlled in both zones by East Germany
	International railways
✈	Airfields
	Army HQ 1945-1949

Canal

FRENCH
SECTOR

TEGEL

Pankow
East German
Government
Capital

Havel
Spree

Heerstrasse
BRITISH
SECTOR

SOVIET

SECTOR

GATOW

TEMPELHOF

Miles
0   5

Dreilinden

Canal
Spree

AMERICAN SECTOR

POPULATION 1962.
West Berlin   2,174,000
East Berlin   603,582

SCHÖNEFELD

118

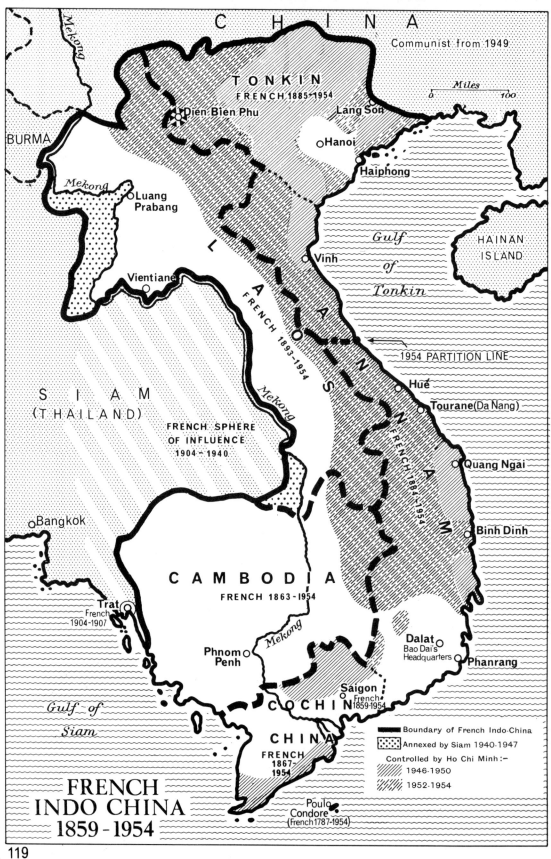

C H I N A

Communist from 1949

T O N K I N
FRENCH 1885-1954

Lang Son

Dien Bien Phu

Hanoi

Haiphong

BURMA

Luang Prabang

Gulf
of
Tonkin

HAINAN
ISLAND

Vientiane

L
A
O
S

FRENCH 1893-1954

Vinh

Miles
0   100

1954 PARTITION LINE

S I A M
(T H A I L A N D)

FRENCH SPHERE
OF INFLUENCE
1904 – 1940

Mekong

Huế

Tourane(Da Nang)

A
N
N
A
M

FRENCH 1884-1954

Quang Ngai

Bangkok

Binh Dinh

C A M B O D I A

FRENCH 1863-1954

Dalat
Bao Dai's
Headquarters

Phanrang

Trat
French
1904-1907

Phnom
Penh

Mekong

Saigon
French
1859-1954

Gulf of
Siam

C O C H I N

CHINA

FRENCH
1867-
1954

Boundary of French Indo-China
Annexed by Siam 1940-1947
Controlled by Ho Chi Minh:-
1946-1950
1952-1954

FRENCH
INDO CHINA
1859-1954

Poulo
Condore
(French 1787-1954)

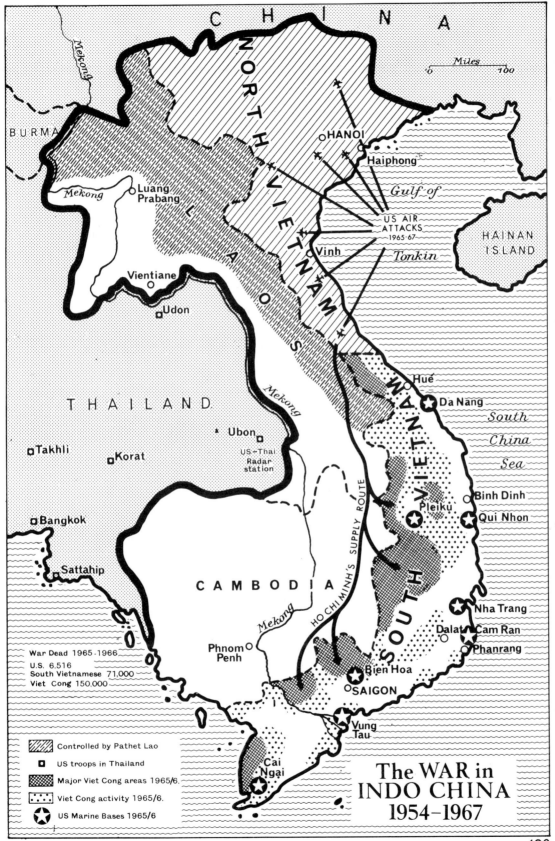

C H I N A

Mekong

BURMA

NORTH VIETNAM

○ HANOI

Haiphong ○

Gulf of

Mekong

LAOS

Luang
Prabang ○

US AIR
ATTACKS
1965·67

HAINAN
ISLAND

Vientiane ○

Vinh ○

Tonkin

△ Udon

THAILAND

Mekong

Hué ○

□ Takhli

◆ Ubon

Da Nang ☆

South

□ Korat

US~Thai
Radar
station

China

Sea

□ Bangkok

Pleiku ☆

Binh Dinh ●

Qui Nhon ☆

● Sattahip

C A M B O D I A

SOUTH VIETNAM

HO CHI MINH'S SUPPLY ROUTE

Nha Trang ☆

Dalat ○

Cam Ran ☆

War Dead 1965-1966
U.S. 6,516
South Vietnamese 71,000
Viet Cong 150,000

Phnom
Penh ○

Mekong

Phanrang ○

Bien Hoa ☆

○ SAIGON

Vung
Tau ☆

Cai
Ngai ☆

The WAR in
INDO CHINA
1954–1967

▨ Controlled by Pathet Lao

□ US troops in Thailand

▨ Major Viet Cong areas 1965/6.

⋯ Viet Cong activity 1965/6.

☆ US Marine Bases 1965/6

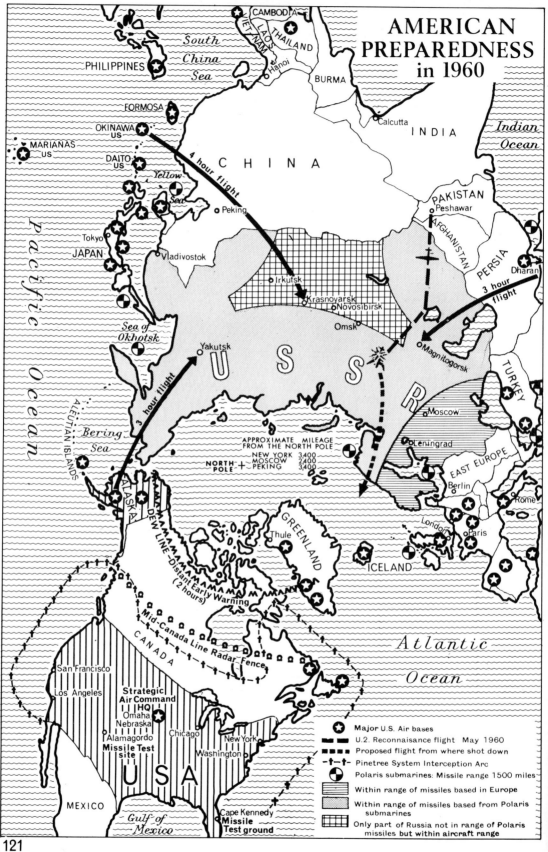

AMERICAN PREPAREDNESS in 1960

CAMBODIA
VIET NAM
LAOS
THAILAND
BURMA
PHILIPPINES
South China Sea
Hanoi
Calcutta
INDIA
Indian Ocean
FORMOSA
OKINAWA US
MARIANAS US
DAITO US
Yellow Sea
C H I N A
PAKISTAN
Peshawar
AFGHANISTAN
PERSIA
Dharan
Tokyo
JAPAN
Peking
Vladivostok
Irkutsk
Krasnoyarsk
Novosibirsk
Omsk
Magnitogorsk
4 hour flight
3 hour flight
TURKEY
Sea of Okhotsk
U S S R
Yakutsk
3 hour flight
Moscow
Leningrad
Pacific Ocean
ALEUTIAN ISLANDS
Bering Sea
APPROXIMATE MILEAGE FROM THE NORTH POLE
NEW YORK 3400
MOSCOW 2400
PEKING 3400
NORTH POLE
EAST EUROPE
Berlin
Rome
London
Paris
ALASKA
DEW LINE-Distant Early Warning (2 hours)
GREENLAND
Thule
ICELAND
Atlantic Ocean
Mid-Canada Line Radar Fence
C A N A D A
San Francisco
Los Angeles
Strategic Air Command HQ
Omaha Nebraska
Chicago
New York
Washington
Alamagordo
Missile Test site
U S A
MEXICO
Gulf of Mexico
Cape Kennedy
Missile Test ground

Major U.S. Air bases
U.2. Reconnaissance flight May 1960
Proposed flight from where shot down
Pinetree System Interception Arc
Polaris submarines: Missile range 1500 miles
Within range of missiles based in Europe
Within range of missiles based from Polaris submarines
Only part of Russia not in range of Polaris missiles but within aircraft range